HARD LABOUR

HARD LABOUR

The Political Diary of
ROBERT KILROY-SILK

CHATTO & WINDUS · LONDON

Published in 1986 by
Chatto & Windus Ltd
40 William IV Street
London WC2N 4DF

British Library Cataloguing in Publication Data

Kilroy-Silk, Robert
  Hard labour.
    1. Great Britain—Politics and
  government—1979-
  I. Title
  320'.092'4   JN237

ISBN 0-7011-3092-X

Photoset by Rowland Phototypesetting Ltd
Bury St Edmunds, Suffolk
Printed by
Redwood Burn Ltd, Trowbridge, Wiltshire

For Dominic and Natasha

'The best lack all conviction, while the worst
Are full of passionate intensity'

W. B. YEATS   *The Second Coming*

Wednesday 25th September 1985

'Your reselection will take place on Tuesday, 10th December,' Peter Killeen said. As assistant regional organiser of the Labour Party in the North West, he was reporting by telephone from Manchester on his meeting with my constituency management committee last night. They voted to start the mandatory reselection process that all Labour MPs now have to face in every Parliament.

At least Peter was positive, if a little dramatic. He made it sound like an execution. There are many who hope that it will be.

'Nominations will close on Thursday, 28th November,' he continued. 'The shortlisting will take place on Tuesday, 3rd December and then reselection the following week.'

'Why is it taking so long?' I asked. It had been informally suggested to me that my 'trial' would be held on 19th November. I had already written the date in my diary and made plans on that basis. I wanted to have the whole thing over and out of the way as quickly as possible, and certainly well before Christmas. My life has already been disrupted and made miserable enough all this last year and more, without prolonging it any longer.

'They wanted more time so that they could consider as wide a field as possible,' Peter Killeen explained. 'Anyway,' he added cheerfully, 'it's not a bad thing. It gives me more time to check on all their credentials.' He will need it. The elegibility of the numerous new Militant-organised delegates will need careful and detailed scrutiny. They'll get it, from me as well as from him.

Jan was dismayed when I told her. Like me, she's tired of the uncertainty and depressed by the constant anxiety about my future, or lack of it. She wants the issue settled. But, unlike me, she still assumes that I will win. Indeed, for her there can be no other outcome, and the result is a foregone conclusion. After all, I've been a dutiful and conscientious MP for the last eleven years.

But it's not as simple as that. Years of service, good or bad, don't count now. What happened to Frank Hooley, the former MP for Sheffield Healey, is a good example of that. Frank was one of the most hardworking and respected of MPs. He had a fine and honourable record on a whole range of important issues – issues often neglected and sometimes unpopular – yet his local party deselected him before the last election.

In any event, my record, like Frank's, is irrelevant. The 'comrades' want someone different. To be fair to them, though bitter experience suggests that it is never wise to be fair to Militants, some of them have always wanted a different kind of MP. That's not unusual, and they have never made any secret about their preferences. A few others joined them after I refused to vote for Tony Benn in the 1981 contest for the deputy leadership of the Labour Party but – with twelve others – abstained. The little group that they comprise has been whispering – they always seem to whisper – and organising against me ever since. That's to be expected.

Yet even at their largest, they were never more than a tiny, though vociferous and abusive minority in the Ormskirk constituency party. They were irritating, no more. We tolerated them, fools and democrats that we were. Things are very different now. The opportunity to extend their influence occurred when the Knowsley North constituency was formed, following the boundary changes that were implemented just before the 1983 general election.

That I lost the chairman, vice-chairman, agent, secretary, treasurer and other officers and supporters, scattered by the Boundary Commissioners to other constituencies, was bad enough. Worse was that the number of Militants in the party was increased substantially by the new areas added to the constituency. Nor were matters helped by the fact that personality differences amongst the moderates, who still had a small majority, and the refusal of each moderate camp to vote for the candidates of the other, resulted in the election of a Militant Tendency supporter as chairman and of his acolytes to other important offices.

They've never looked back. They are still only a minority in the party, and until a month or so ago, when there was a sudden and massive influx of new delegates, they were still a minority on the constituency management committee. But they now control it. They're the largest single group. They meet beforehand to determine their line, and then act as a disciplined force. Voting as a block encourages some of the 'neutrals' to support them, whilst deterring others from opposing them. Their mere existence is intimidating, certainly in a political sense, for they're a formidable group to be reckoned with by anyone who wants to be elected to office in the constituency party, delegated to the district party, or even selected as a candidate for the council. They're also, of course, physically intimidating. And they know it. They're not afraid to use their power either. If they can put together enough votes they will select a Militant to replace me.

At one time, earlier in the year, I felt inclined to let them have their way. I confided as much to Tony Bevins. Although he's the political correspondent of *The Times*, he's my oldest and best friend. We met as impoverished students at the LSE in 1961.

'They want a different kind of MP,' I told Tony. 'They want a duffel-coated unshaven revolutionary, who'll spend most of his time at the end of a megaphone on every conceivable demonstration and who'd wallow in the notoriety and glamour of being arrested on a picket line. That's not me. And I'm not prepared to be like that.'

'Maybe,' Tony said. 'But that's not what your voters want, or even your ordinary party members. They want to be represented by someone like you.'

He was right. The proof was there in the 25,000 people who voted for me at the last election and who gave me a 17,000-plus majority. But that's of no account. The constituency party want someone different, or rather the small but well-organised, active and vociferous minority do. And, in the end, that is what will count.

So, despite Tony's worried protestations, I decided that if it became the clearly-expressed view of my constituency management committee as presently constituted that they preferred another candidate, then I would accept the decision with as much dignity and good grace as I could muster and quietly step aside.

But now I've changed my mind. I've no intention of going quietly, like Frank Hooley. The intervention of Bob Parry, the MP for Liverpool Riverside, changed all that.

One night in May he sidled up to me in his hangdog fashion, just as I was about to vote in the 'Aye' lobby in the House of Commons.

'Bob,' he whispered. He glanced around conspiratorially as if to ensure that no-one was listening. 'Can I have a word?' He beckoned me to the desk in the alcove directly opposite the place where the two clerks in their high Victorian-style desks were ticking off the names of MPs as they filed past and voted. 'I've been asked to have a word with you, as chairman of the group.' He coughed. He meant the Merseyside Group of Labour MPs – which did not meet very often and the identity of whose chairman was unknown even to some members of the group. He seemed hesitant – conscious, I assumed, that I was not giving him my full attention. I was impatient to vote and leave for home.

'I've a . . .' He looked round again. 'I've been asked to offer you a deal,' he said. I listened, first with incredulity, then amazement, and finally with a mixture of anxiety and anger, of which the latter predominated.

What the 'deal' amounted to was that I should reconcile myself to the 'fact' that I would not be reselected for my Knowsley North seat and that I would be replaced by the Militant supporter and President of Liverpool Labour Party, Tony Mulhearn. That, he said, had already been 'decided'. However, if I went quietly and there was 'no fuss', then I could have the candidature for the neighbouring, but Tory-held, West Lancashire constituency. We should win this seat at the next election, he said, especially if I was the candidate, as it was composed of a large part of my old Ormskirk constituency which had been taken away by the 1983 boundary changes. If, however, I refused to accept 'reality' and caused a public row, I would find myself blacklisted in West Lancashire and elsewhere as well as deselected in Knowsley North.

All this, apparently, was 'decided' – he kept using the word – at a secret caucus meeting at the Transport and General Workers Union office in Transport House, Liverpool, following a caucus of the so-called 'broad left' that chose Mulhearn to be their candidate in preference to Keva Coombes, the Leader of Merseyside County Council, and Jim Lloyd, the Leader of my own Knowsley Council.

It is no secret that all three have an interest in securing the nomination for my seat. Jim Lloyd tried to get the candidature in Sean Hughes' seat of Knowsley South and again in Knowsley North in 1983. He failed on both occasions. Since then, however, he has assiduously sought support in my party. Keva Coombes and Tony Mulhearn are after seats wherever they might be found and wherever a chance might present itself. Both were at one time active in trying to replace Frank Field in Birkenhead. Both failed. Indeed, Tony Mulhearn was on the short-list when I was selected for Ormskirk in 1973. He put his head in his hands and cried when told that I had won on the first ballot and that he had only received one vote.

The meeting, as I learned later, had indeed taken place but was, characteristically, manipulated by Militant. This led to Coombes and Lloyd, the latter of whom had not been present, refusing to abide by its decision.

When I did not hug him thankfully for his help and statesmanship, but actually abused him for being prepared to be involved in such a 'deal', Bob Parry was genuinely surprised. He obviously saw himself not as a mere messenger, but as a fixer, a conciliator, an arbitrator. He tried to persuade me to accept the bargain: he really believed that it would be in my best interests. And this from a parliamentary colleague. 'Give up your seat, Bob,' he was saying, in effect, 'and be a good boy about it and go quietly.'

Like hell.

He seemed upset when I called him a creep. 'You're doing Militant's dirty work for it,' I added. 'You're just as bad as them. Well, you can tell them that there's no way that I'll go quietly. There'll be a god-almighty row.'

'But . . .' he persisted, shoulders stooped, hands like Uriah Heep.

'Piss off,' I suggested. I gave my name to the clerk, bowed to the whips at the exit of the Lobby where they were counting, and left.

I couldn't be bothered to talk to him any more. The fact that he hadn't anticipated my reaction – still less understood it – made any further conversation a waste of time. I would have expected a fellow MP to have refused to deliver such a message and, indeed, to warn me about what was happening.

I couldn't wait to tell my colleagues what Parry had said. I told as many as I could, especially the inveterate gossips, which actually means all MPs. Like me they were amazed that such a deal could have been concocted, and were equally contemptuous of Parry for being the messenger boy. For weeks afterwards the poor sod was approached by colleagues enquiring in mock trepidation if he had got a 'deal' for them too.

This offer of a 'deal' made me determined to fight. It was a decision that was strongly endorsed by Jan and, later, by Neil Kinnock. A few weeks after the encounter with Parry, when it had all become public, I offered Neil my resignation from the front bench Home Office team. I thought that it might be more damaging for the party if a frontbencher were seen to be in conflict with his local party than would be the case for a backbencher. Neil insisted that I stay.

Jan also, as usual, saw the brighter side. 'Actually,' she said, when her initial anger had subsided, 'it's a compliment. They're saying that they couldn't win Tory West Lancashire but that you can. They're admitting that you're the better and stronger candidate and more acceptable to the public. They need the cushion of your 17,000 majority in order to get elected.' It was a good point. I used it a great deal in the subsequent radio and television interviews on the subject.

I wanted to make the Parry 'deal' public, and to inform a wider audience about the machinations of Militant and of the shenanigans in Knowsley North. I had to do no more than report the whole episode to the next meeting of my constituency party, as indeed it was reasonable that I should: someone, I knew, would leak it to the press. Someone always leaked stories like this – and this was a good one in press terms. And the press even got it right, both in the *Liverpool Echo* and, a couple of days later, in *The Times* and the *Guardian*.

At the May consituency meeting, instead of making my normal parliamentary report at the end of the evening, I delivered a short statement recounting the offer of the 'deal'. I went on to say that I found the whole thing extraordinary and that whilst I was prepared to be judged on my record and to accept their decision, I was not prepared to allow the local party to be hijacked and manipulated by a secret caucus operating in Liverpool. I refused to be intimidated, I would fight with all the strength at my disposal, and I expected their support.

I did not, however, name Parry. My main motive, I admit, was to ensure that the story ran in the press for a few days longer than it would otherwise have done. I thought that would be helpful to me, and so it was. A hunt began in the local Liverpool newspapers and on local radio and television for the 'mystery MP'; the Merseyside MPs, led by the Militant supporter and MP for neighbouring Broadgreen, Terry Fields, all fell over themselves to say 'It wasn't me'.

Big-mouth Fields, not the brightest of MPs, rushed to report to *The Times* that I was telling 'fairy tales' and 'scare stories'. I was pleased to hear that he knew more than I did. It was a relief to be told, even via the columns of the 'capitalist press', that I was not faced with a Militant-organised campaign to deselect me and that I had indulged in 'fairy tales'. But I was right and he was wrong.

After he'd made a statement to the press, he telephoned me.

'It wasn't me,' he asserted.

'I know that,' I agreed.

'Oh.' He sounded non-plussed. All the aggression that I had felt down the telephone line seemed to have disappeared. He appeared to be having difficulty in understanding, so I explained.

'*I* know it wasn't you, Terry,' I said. 'And *you* know it wasn't you. So it wasn't you.'

There was a long pause, then he said, 'Oh, but everyone thinks it's me.'

'Well then,' I said reassuringly. 'You can say that you've spoken to me and I've agreed that you should say what we both know to be true: it wasn't you.'

'I can say that?'

'Yes.'

'Great.'

That pleased him enormously. He went off like someone who'd just found a stand ticket for a Liverpool v. Everton Cup Final.

I also refused to name Parry as the go-between in order to protect him. I know that sounds strange, but it's nevertheless true. Even with hindsight I can remember feeling that I ought not to divulge his name because he had spoken to me in confidence. Perhaps that kind of naivety, or whatever it is, demonstrates that I'm not a real get-'em-by-the-throat politician and that I don't deserve to survive. Anyway, I didn't name him. It leaked out.

But back to the May meeting. Immediately I had finished my statement and sat down there was uproar. That's what I'd anticipated. But you would have expected, wouldn't you, that the bitterness and the anger would have been directed at the conspirators and their messenger-boy? Not a bit of it. The normal rules of civilised behaviour don't apply when Militant is in control. Their fury and abuse was directed at me. Indeed, those I knew to have been a part of the caucus and to be supporters of Militant were the loudest and the crudest in their condemnation of me. And for what? For not naming Parry. I was censured for this omission at the next meeting in June. I felt as if I had just been mugged and on reporting the matter to the police had been rewarded with a hard kick in the guts.

From that point, however, they no longer pretended that they were not engaged in an attempt to have a Militant, or someone who would dance to its tune, representing Knowsley North.

In July 1984 the then Secretary of State for the Environment, Patrick Jenkin, said in an interview on Merseyside's *Radio City* that

Liverpool City Council had backed away from the brink of bankruptcy because it would destroy the ambition of Derek Hatton, the deputy leader of the City Council, to become an MP. Jenkin also said that Hatton was lined up for my seat. My Militant supporter chairman, Jim McGinley, scuttled along to the local press to deny that there was any foundation in the story. 'Members of Knowsley North,' he had said, 'have expressed their full support for Mr Kilroy-Silk.'

Peter Fisher, a young docker, local councillor, my ex-parliamentary agent and still a friend and confidant, warned me at the time not to be misled by the statement. 'That's what the chairmen of second-rate football clubs say about their managers, Robert,' he scoffed, 'before they sack them.' And it was.

Throughout the summer of 1985 a state of open warfare existed in the constituency party, with my management committee clearly divided between the pro- and the anti-Militants. There was no room in the middle. Those that tried to be all things to all men, and there were still a few, merely helped to strengthen the power of the Militants.

Not being political fanatics, and having their own lives to lead, my supporters do not attend meetings as diligently as the Militants do. That has to be admitted. But it also has to be said that when they do attend they have to brazen out an aggressively hostile atmosphere, endure being hissed at, heckled and jeered at every time they speak, especially if what they say is not in line with Militant dogma. At times, they are even physically intimidated. This applies to the elderly women as much as to the men. Indeed, some of the bravest and outspoken of the 'real' Labour party member are retired ladies. They've got real guts. But the way they are treated is, of course, one of the reasons why others don't always attend when they should. Indeed, there are many good, loyal and long-serving members of the party who have stopped coming to meetings altogether because of the way that they are treated by their 'comrades'.

'There's no point,' they say. 'We're never allowed to speak. And when we are we're just shouted down.'

They know that this is defeatist, that it simply plays into the hands of the Militants. They know they are giving the party to the Militants. But it is difficult to persuade them that their duty requires them to turn up on a wet Tuesday evening in the winter to sit in a cold room to be reviled and shouted at by political thugs. They won't do it. It's like Gresham's law of money: the bad drives out the good.

So a clear field is left for the Militants. Their position on the management committee has also been strengthened by a sudden increase in the number of delegates. These have been stable at around 80 for the last couple of years, indeed longer. Now there are 140.

It's interesting to work out how they've achieved this. Like all others, my constituency Labour party is governed by a management committee that usually meets once a month. It is this committee that selects the parliamentary candidate and to which he or she is responsible. The committee is composed of delegates, elected by the branches of the party organised at the level of each local council ward in the constituency. There are ten such wards, and therefore branches of the party, in my constituency. Each one of these sends its secretary and two delegates to the constituency management committee for their first 50 members, or part thereof, and one additional delegate for each additional 50 members, or part thereof, with a maximum of ten delegates from any one branch. Most of the wards or branches, especially those controlled by the Militant, have fewer than 50 members and have, therefore, just three delegates.

In addition, each organisation affiliated to the Labour party that has members living in the constituency can accredit delegates on the basis of one delegate per 100 members, or part thereof, with a maximum of five delegates from any one branch. These organisations are usually trade unions, but they also include such bodies as the Fabian Society, the Co-operative Party, the Society of Labour Lawyers, and the Socialist Medical Association.

The increase in the number of delegates has occurred in this latter category. An increase in delegates from the local branches of the party could only have been obtained by the recruitment of more members, but an increase from the trade union section could be achieved simply by persuading those union branches that were not members of the local party to affiliate and to send delegates on the basis of their membership. As this would often be in the hundreds, unlike that of the local parties, it provides great scope for a sudden increase in the number of delegates.

Some of the new delegates are, thankfully, ordinary long-standing members of the party, and if not supporters of mine then certainly anti-Militants; alarmed by Militant's activity in the constituency,

9

they have taken up their trade union delegate's credentials in order to support me.

Many, it seemed like dozens, have appeared as if from nowhere. Most of them come under the auspices of the Transport and General Workers Union. They are self-conscious, but arrogantly so. They sit together in a large group, smirking. It's obvious that they have all been recruited by the Militants. They've little or no idea of how meetings are conducted and still less of what the Labour party is and stands for. I don't believe that they are socialists. They certainly do not value democracy. They openly take instructions on how to vote from the Militants and enthusiastically join in the jeering and heckling of the other delegates. They treat the meetings as a joke.

It is the credentials of all these that need to be carefully scrutinised: I'm sure that many will be found to be invalid. Long-established members of the party, councillors and Justices of the Peace who live in the same wards as some of these delegates claim to be from, swear that they have never seen them before. Yet here they are, on the management committee of one of the safest Labour seats in England and about to decide who shall be its next MP.

Today I asked Peter Killeen for the final list of delegates that he was given last night by the constituency secretary, Cathy Toner. I want to 'go through the list with a fine toothcomb', as my parliamentary colleagues have all enjoined me to do, to ensure that the delegates are all eligible to vote in the reselection. To be eligible they have to live in the constituency, to have been a member of the constituency party the previous year, have paid their subscription and, if representing trade unions or other affiliated organisations, have been properly nominated.

Peter hesitated.

'What's the matter, Peter?' I asked. I was sitting at my desk in the bay window of my study. A green woodpecker was picking ants off the warm lawn.

'Well, I'm not sure,' he said quietly.

'What d'you mean, you're not sure? I'm the bloody MP, for God's sake. I'm entitled to have a full and up-to-date and accurate list of the delegates.'

And so I am. The only reason I didn't have one already was that the constituency secretary, Cathy Toner, is a supporter of the Militants. She works hand-in-glove with them, and always finds good reasons why an up-to-date list is not available. Mind you, given the way in which new delegates have appeared in the last couple of months, this isn't surprising.

What was surprising, on this occasion, was to have the assistant regional organiser of the party hesitate about letting me have a copy of the list of those able to make the selection. If he is going to be ultra-cautious and proper then I am in more trouble than I thought I was. Peter left the phone to seek advice. The woodpecker flew away. When Peter came back, he said he'd send me the list.

Now the long, boring, painstaking but crucial task of examining all the delegates' credentials can begin. The detective work of my voluntary agent, Geoff Kneale, who works full-time as a Post Office Engineer, will be crucial. So will that of Peter Fisher, especially in relation to the Transport and General Workers' Union, of which he is an active member. He has good contacts there. Only when their work has been completed, and those not eligible to vote have been eliminated, will we be able to make a count. At that point we will know who is going to win.

Of course, I don't really believe that I will lose. I'm sure deep down that something will happen; something, as they say, will 'turn up'. It's inconceivable, after all, that I could be defeated, that I won't be an MP.

But in reality I know otherwise. It could happen. In my coldly analytical moments I think that I've already adjusted to the fact that I won't be in the next Parliament. In some ways I'm not even sure that I want to be. The last couple of years, and particularly this summer, have been difficult and miserable. The public debate about my political future and the constant enquiries from the media and acquaintances is tedious and distasteful. I'm sick of it. And now I face the prospect of more public conflict, acrimony and even humil-iation.

Naturally I'm worried about my own reputation, my own image. After all, the impartial man in the street will think there must be something wrong with the bloke if they want to get rid of him. But I'm also concerned about the effect on Jan and the kids. They're wonderful – as supportive as anyone could want. They pretend not to be anxious, and that it doesn't get to them. But it does, especially to Jan, though she disguises it well. Our summer was virtually destroyed by it, apart from a few idyllic days in a villa high in the hills of Tuscany near Babisccio, with Ruth Jackson, a director for the BBC TV *Forty Minutes* programme, and Guy East, a director of

Goldcrest, and later Duncan Heath, an agent for a famous American film star who seemed to spend most of the time on the radio-phone to California saying, 'She won't even begin talking under four million. . . .' We spent a couple of days in the enchantment that's Siena, but Florence, hot, dusty, dirty and backpack-dominated, was a disappointment in comparison with our memory of it as students twenty years ago. This year's holiday was our first without the kids, who'd refused to accompany us. Even though Dominic is eighteen and Natasha is sixteen, Jan is worried about them; I worried about the state the house would be in when we got back. Knowing Natasha, I knew there would be parties every night.

But I'm depressed politically. I keep asking myself why we're all silent while Scargill and the mad Liverpool Militants present themselves as the only face of socialism and the Labour movement. The TUC has already capitulated. Only the brave Norman Willis dared to defy the new, vulgar, vile double standards that masquerade as socialism. So now we're in favour of the next Labour Government legislating to review all the cases of the miners gaoled during the course of the dispute, reinstating those who have been sacked, and reimbursing the NUM for all the money that has been confiscated by fines, sequestration and receivership.

Well I'm not in favour of it, and I won't vote for it. It's a nonsense. Those miners who are in prison have been tried, convicted and sentenced by the ordinary courts in the normal way and they, like everyone else, have to accept the consequences of their actions. No Labour Government should say anything else. If mistakes have been made, and that is always possible, then they have to be rectified by the normal legal procedures that apply to everyone. In any case, why should it be only the miners who have their cases 'reviewed'? What about other individuals convicted of the same offence during the dispute, or other trade unionists convicted before or since of the same offence, while in pursuit of industrial action: are their cases also to be 'reviewed'? And why stop there? What about every other person currently in prison convicted of the same offence: why are their cases of assault or criminal damage any less worthy of review? And in any event, if the law and the courts cannot be trusted in these cases why can they be trusted in any other? But Scargill is selective. He and his union are happy enough to use the 'capitalist laws' and the 'Tory Courts' on other occasions.

As for the money that the union has lost – squandered would be a more apt description – we're told by Scargill that it has been confiscated by the courts as a result of the operation of Tory laws. That's not true. It's been dissipated because the NUM leadership would not abide by the common and civil law of the country that applies to everyone else. Fine. That's their decision. They're entitled to it. But they must be prepared to pay the price and not come squealing to a Labour Government asking to be retrospectively indemnified, or if they do then they must be told to get lost.

No-one is pointing out that to undermine the judicial system and the law in this way will eventually be detrimental to the unions and to their members. It is our people, those that voted for me and whom I represent, who will lose out the most. They need laws that outlaw social injustice and oppression, that keep in check the rapacious appetites and instincts of the powerful and give positive legal rights to the poor, the inarticulate and the unorganised. Above all, they need a society in which these laws are both respected and obeyed. Anyone, Arthur Scargill included, who undermines the law does a great disservice to working people. They don't seem to understand that, 'Wherever law ends, Tyranny begins.' Or perhaps they do.

I wrote all that in my fortnightly column in *Police Review*, in the issue that appeared on 13th September. I told the truth and I felt I'd been courageous. That is a measure of how crazy our world has become, how warped the values that are now being paraded, the double-speak we're subjected to. And the fear. We're all afraid to speak out, to tell the truth.

I'm sure, I know, what most of my colleagues think, even though we're still in the middle of the long recess, and not in communication. I know what they think because I've worked with them for the last dozen years, I've heard them privately and I know their values are much the same as mine. But they're silent, because they don't want to jeopardise their own position or, more charitably, do not want to divide the party and add to the conflict. The last consideration is an important and respectable one, but it's misguided. It means that those who do all the shouting – in this instance, Scargill and the Liverpool Militants – are allowed to have it all their own way. So far as the general public is concerned they are the face and the voice of the Labour Party.

What is worse is that our failure to give a lead and to oppose such lunacy means that the silent majority of Labour members and voters who disagree with Scargill and the Militants is left unrepresented, without a voice. They begin to believe that what the street and mob orators are saying is acceptable and respectable. It becomes more respectable the longer it remains uncontradicted. And so their numbers will swell. When and if action is taken to counter all this it could well be too late.

It already is too late in Liverpool. What is happening there would have all the elements of a pantomime – certainly street theatre – were the consequences not so serious for ordinary working people. The Militants say that they have budgeted for a deficit and are campaigning to protect jobs and services, yet their actions have put both in jeopardy. Indeed, we now have the bizarre situation that, having called a meeting of the council to issue redundancy notices to the council's 30,000 workforce, the political cowards that call themselves Labour councillors retreated as soon as they were confronted by a picket line. Not only that. They joined the picket. And even then the farce continued. Not content with picketing themselves they then applauded the pickets, which now included themselves, for preventing them from attending the meeting.

God help us. And then we expect people to vote Labour. Now they and the joint shop steward committee are calling for an indefinite strike. It's crazy. They think it will force the Government to give them the money they've already been refused. It won't. Kenneth Baker, the Secretary of State for the Environment, won't allow himself to be out-manoeuvred and humiliated like Patrick Jenkin was last year. The strike will merely penalise the people of Liverpool. It will cut off their services and destroy their jobs – both the things that Militant are supposed to be protecting.

I can't think of much that's more reprehensible than what is now happening in Liverpool. The Militants are actually demanding that council employees go on strike so that the council won't have to pay their wages. The Council will therefore not go bankrupt, or at least not yet, and the councillors will not have to make a humiliating climb-down. They will even be able to claim a victory. But the victory, if it comes on these terms, will have been at the expense of those who will have gone without their wages and been denied council services. The most poor and the most vulnerable will, as always, be the greatest sufferers.

It's a bloody disgrace that they should be allowed to play with people's lives and jobs like this. At least Jack Cunningham is fighting back. He was on *The World at One* yesterday. He was good – firm, honest, forthright – as he always is. But it should have been done sooner and more often and by more of us.

Earlier in the week, I can't now remember which day, I was in the garden changing the water for the ducks and geese. It was very hot and quiet. Something had been on the radio about Scargill's attempt to railroad next week's Labour Party conference into accepting his demands. I was angry and frustrated at what was happening. I was standing watching the immaculate white geese that I'd bred picking the corn from the hard ground when Jan arrived. She leaned on the wide white metal gate.

'I'm going to make a statement,' I said. She knew what I meant, as we've talked about it a great deal. She shares my anger and disgust at what is happening. I told her that if I didn't speak out I would have a heart attack. That is how it feels. I actually have a deep burning pain in the middle of my chest. 'This isn't what I came into politics for,' I said. 'I didn't come into politics to support lies and bullying and intimidation and law-breaking. That's not me.'

'You're not supporting them,' she said consolingly.

'But I am if I don't speak out. My silence is tantamount to approval.'

I let the hosepipe drop and leaned on the gate alongside her. The ducks paddled in the pool of water that was forming.

'All right,' she said. 'Do it. But why you? What are all the rest doing?' She named names. 'They've been reselected. They're safe. They can do it from a position of strength. They'd even have their constituency party supporting them. You wouldn't.' She continued quietly, hesitating, searching for the word. 'You're the most *vulnerable*. You've the most to lose.'

She was right.

'Ring Neil,' she said. 'Tell him how you feel. He must feel the same. He thinks like you. He hates the shits. Tell him to speak out. He needs to know,' she added, 'that that's how you feel, and that you'll support him. He probably feels isolated too.'

We walked back to the house.

'Do what you want to,' she said. 'Do what makes you feel best.'

And I've done nothing. That's why they are winning.

Thursday 26th September 1985

The list of delegates arrived. It looks bad. There are now 141 delegates, which means I need the votes of 71 in order to win. A quick count and I reckon I've got 64, with another ten possibles. That's not enough. Even assuming that all the 'possibles' voted for me, it's too tight – I can't rely on them all turning up on the night.

But this is just the beginning. A cursory examination shows that three of my supporters are missing. Two were recently nominated by the Electricians' Union and were both at the last meeting of the management committee on Tuesday, when the secretary announced that they had been nominated. According to Peter Killeen that means they're OK to vote. Another is Phil McSorley, a long-standing T & G delegate, a retired docker and a wit, who has constantly insisted that he has been nominated as a delegate by his branch but has never received notice of meetings. This means there are 144 delegates, that I need 73 to win, and that I now have 67. Moreover, Peter Killeen says that two others have to be knocked off as everyone agrees they aren't eligible – one of them a full-time officer of the T & G who has not been a member of the party for the last two years. I had put him down as being against me. The other, unfortunately, I had counted as being for me.

So now we have 142 delegates, I need 72, and I have 66. But still we have not finished. According to Peter Killeen there are more delegates from the Transport and General Workers Union than it has paid affiliations for. He reckons that at least eight, and possibly a dozen, will have to go. That's good news, since they're the ones that have suddenly appeared as if from nowhere and who do the bidding of the chairman and the other Militants. Even more delegates are suspect on other grounds, particularly three new delegates that have arrived from ASTMS, another from the Trades Council and still more from the T & G.

I spoke to Peter Fisher on the telephone. 'It looks bad,' I said. He wasn't worried. He was confident we would find that enough of the new delegates were not eligible to vote and that I would win. He's excited by the challenge and was anxious to begin the careful and discreet investigation of the qualifications of the delegates. I gave him a long list of names and addresses and union affiliations that

16

need to be checked out. I also posted him a copy of the full list.

My agent, Geoff Kneale, is also keen to begin the detective work. So is his wife, the Mayor of Knowsley, Frances Kneale. Like Peter Fisher, they seem to be animated by the promise of defeating the Militants. I hope that their excitement and confidence will be rewarded. I'm in trouble if they're not.

Friday 27th – Sunday 29th September 1985

The Liverpool Militants dominate all political conversations. They have been defeated over the strike call but intend to go ahead with a one-day stoppage. Tony Byrne, the chairman of the Finance Committee, continued to pledge that there would be no redundancies amongst the 31,000 workforce and no cuts in services – but that was on Wednesday, I think. Now they've decided to issue all their workers with redundancy notices to take effect on 31st December. They're mad.

Dave Montgomery, an old friend who acted as my press officer when I was first elected in February 1974, and is now the editor of the *News of the World*, also thinks they're mad. He also believes there are more sinister things in the background. On Thursday we had tea sitting on the sofa in his large office in Bouverie Street. He told me that his journalists have been investigating Hatton.

They know a great deal about him. They know his income and where he banks, how much he paid for his house, his clothes, his daughter's pony and her riding lessons. They know which 'expensive' restaurants he dines at and the clubs to which he belongs.

'So?' I said, unimpressed.

'It'll kill him off,' David said. He looked surprised by my complacent reaction. 'It will destroy him politically.'

'I doubt it.' I really did. I'd like to believe that it was true, not just because I would like to see Hatton 'killed off', although of course I would. He's doing more damage to Liverpool than Hitler ever contrived. He's damaging the Labour party and our electoral prospects to a greater extent than Benn and Scargill, and that's saying something. I'd also like to see him 'killed off' politically because we need to show that the Labour party will have no truck with the superficial political philosophy and the hectoring and intimidatory style of street politics that he represents.

But it won't happen. The rules have altered. Things that were totally unacceptable to decent Labour voters and party members a few years ago probably still aren't acceptable, but they seem to be tolerated by the activists. In any case, Hatton shouldn't be politically arraigned for his sharp clothes and his daughter's riding lessons.

Tony Bevins is just as preoccupied with Militant, but then he has good cause. He's been in Liverpool all week covering the developing crisis in the city for *The Times*. Tony comes from Liverpool; his parents and a brother still live there. He knows and loves the place.

I've been conscious during my conversations with him throughout the year that he didn't really believe what I was saying about the way in which the Militants behave either in my constituency or in Liverpool. I could tell that he thought I was exaggerating just a little when I spoke of the constant allegations of corruption, the intimidation, the atmosphere of fear that has been created, and of how otherwise brave party members are physically afraid. 'Poor Rob,' I could see him thinking. 'It's really getting to him.'

He rang me from Liverpool earlier this week. It was after midnight. 'You were right,' he said, without even a preliminary hello. 'It's terrible.'

Today, Saturday, he sat with Jan and me in the sun in the garden retelling the horrors of his week covering the Liverpool saga: the streets full of heavy-booted, unshaven, beer-swigging youths, their coats covered in badges, many of them from other parts of the country; the press manipulated and television crews and reporters physically intimidated. He also hated the way in which political conversations are conducted in whispers to add to the sense of drama and conspiracy.

'They all whisper,' he said. 'All the time. It's incredible. They whisper in the streets, in the council building and in the pubs. They go up to each other, put their hand across their mouth and whisper in the other person's ear. I'm so stupid,' he laughed, 'I thought it was sexual.'

Michael Cockerell, a reporter for BBC TV, is also interested in Militant. He wants to make a film about my reselection difficulties for the BBC Sunday lunchtime programme, *This Week, Next Week*. He has rung me several times in the last few days but I've tried to put him off.

I don't want to do it. I don't feel up to all the time and trouble and aggravation that will be involved. I don't even want to explain, yet again, why it is they want to get rid of me. It's becoming both boring and debilitating. But I suppose he will make the film whether I co-operate or not, so it's better to make sure that my case comes across. I've agreed to have lunch with him in Bournemouth. At least he's chosen a restaurant from *The Good Food Guide*.

The one bright spot of the weekend, except for the glorious Indian summer and fine gardening weather, was Liverpool's defeat of Tottenham Hotspur by four goals to one. Manchester United, unfortunately, also won: they beat Southampton 1:0, so we're still nine points adrift of them at the top of the League. The good thing is that they both beat southern clubs.

Monday 30th September 1985

Before leaving home with Jan for Bournemouth and the Conference, I cleared my desk of all correspondence, including the letters that Sarah Lawrence, my secretary, delivered this morning. It's a great advantage that she lives nearby. It means that she can collect and deliver work at weekends and during the parliamentary recesses.

Today's post was, as always, dominated by letters from constituents requesting a transfer from a flat or maisonette to a house. It really is a disgrace that so many young couples with small children are still imprisoned in tiny and inadequate multi-story flats. Apart from unemployment, and the poverty and distress that accompany it, especially in the case of the long-term unemployed (of whom there are a great many in Knowsley), housing is the major problem. That this should be the case, that there should be so many complaints about the need for repairs when most of the property is new, is not much of a testimony to the competence or imagination of our architects and planners.

It's not surprising that I identify closely with my constituents and their problems. After all, my mother and all the rest of my family live in similar conditions and in the same kind of council houses in Birmingham. Moreover, it's not really all that long since I left the slums of Birmingham. I can vividly recall the tiny, damp back-to-back in Buckingham Street with one room downstairs and two up. There was no such luxury as a bathroom; instead, we had a tin bath in front of a coal fire under gas lights on Friday evenings or – a great and special treat – a trip to the local public baths in George Street where scalding hot water gushed from wide taps turned on with a key by the attendant. Our lavatory was something different. That was in the yard and shared with six other families, not all of whom were as clean as we would have liked.

A Labour council and the welfare state rescued my family and most of my constituents from these conditions. Yet whilst the amenities have improved the physical structure of the new houses is frequently shoddy and the environment soul-destroying.

There are also some letters from prisoners. I probably receive about a dozen a week in my capacity as Chairman of the All-Party Parliamentary Penal Affairs Group. Many of the prisoners, like some of my constituents, have a multiplicity of problems and develop a new one just as soon as I've solved the old one. They become regular correspondents.

When dealing with complaints from people like Myra Hindley, Stuart Blackstock or Charles Richardson, I try not to think about what they have done – just that they are being punished by being deprived of their liberty and that they are otherwise entitled to be treated decently. It's hard though, especially when, for example, I have a clear picture in my mind's eye of Blackstock's victim, P.C. Olds, and the horrible contraptions that he has to employ in order to walk after being wounded by Blackstock. But I take all their complaints seriously. With the help of Paul Cavadino, the part-time clerk to the group, I investigate all their allegations. I also follow up everything they tell me, because in the nature of the people that I am dealing with it would be foolish to take chances.

One prisoner, John Smith, wrote to me and said that when he got out of prison he would kill Judge Openshaw, the Senior Circuit Judge at Preston Crown Court who had sentenced him to 18 months' borstal 13 years ago. He carried out the threat. Then, at his trial for murder, he said that he had warned me of what he proposed to do. The implication was that I had done nothing and that if I had acted I could have prevented the murder. Fortunately, although I probably didn't take him seriously, I had learnt enough to pass the information on to the police. I still have carbons of my letters.

Nor was he the only one to mean what he said. A prisoner in Walton Prison, Liverpool, wrote asking for help, claiming that he was being victimised. He killed himself by cutting his wrists with a razor two weeks after I alerted the Home Secretary to his threat. I felt responsible for his death, even though I had done all that I could to prevent it. The man had mentioned in his letter that he had already attempted to take his life and that he had been in Rampton Hospital. Yet in spite of the fact that the prison authorities should have known about his problem and should have been further alerted when the censor read his letter to me and again when I wrote to the Minister, they still failed him. The fact that he was mentally ill and should not have been in prison in the first place only compounded our collective failure.

A similar thing happened with Stuart Blackstock. I received an eight-page letter from him alleging ill-treatment and saying that he wanted to remain alone in the punishment block in Leeds prison and that he would attack prison officers and take hostages if he was manhandled again. He told me that he had a bit of steel out of which he had made a knife and that the prison officers had searched his cell but had not found it. Besides writing back to him saying that I was looking into his allegations and telling him to give the knife up, I also, of course, warned the Home Office of what he had said. I imagined they had already read his letter to me and knew about it, but perhaps they hadn't. It was, after all, atrocious handwriting, worse than mine, and it did take up eight pages of large fine-lined notepaper. He was later charged with possessing a knife and attempting to take a prison officer hostage.

So, rushed and late as we were, I read all the letters carefully, leaving instructions for Paul as to how to deal with them.

I also spoke at length to Peter Fisher. He already had a copy of the list of delegates, and I wanted to be sure that we were both thinking and working along the same lines. Over the weekend I was looking at the names and organisations of the new delegates. Even a stranger casting a cursory eye over the five printed pages would see that there is something strange about the number of Transport and General Workers' Union branches and delegates that are now affiliated.

The T & G in the North West is clearly at the centre of an attempt to manipulate the selection process. What is amazing is that it's so blatant. Either the Militants are now so arrogant that they don't care if they're rumbled, or so incompetent that they can't see it for themselves. It's the former, of course. More important is that either the union has allowed itself to be manipulated or the nominations and the delegates are invalid.

I hope it's the latter. Not just because it would both show up the Militants and their arrogance and incompetence and discredit them – as well, of course, as helping my reselection – but because the T & G is my union. I have been a member of it ever since I was first eligible to join a union on starting work. I'd hate to think it was involved in something like this at any official level. Indeed, the only reason I feel at all confident today is that I know that when Peter Fisher has done his detective work the union will act to sort it out.

Meanwhile, the facts are straightforward. We have always had only a handful of T & G branches affiliated to the constituency party. This was also true of the old Ormskirk constituency. The branches have remained the same year in and year out for the last dozen years. So, in the main, have their delegates. Thus, at the Annual General Meeting earlier this year we had four T & G branches with a total of fifteen delegates. Now, however, there are fifteen T & G branches with a total of thirty-six delegates, and most of these have appeared suddenly in the last two months.

We don't know where some of these branches are supposed to be located. On the list of organisations affiliated to the constituency party the T & G branches are designated simply by a number. So 6/556, for example, is listed together with the names of its four delegates, but we know where the branch is because it's been affiliated for a long time. It's the Pendletons ice cream factory branch in Kirkby. But what are 6/636, 6/536, 6/642 or 6/636, and where the hell is 5/518? I ask Peter to find out.

'It's probably a mistake,' he says. 'A typing error.'

It probably is. There are lots of those, too, and some of them are important. Am I becoming paranoid?

We also need to know who all the 'new' delegates are. This means ensuring that they are on the electoral register and actually live at the address that they have given. Are they members of the party and have they been so for the requisite twelve months?

And then, just to make sure we've examined every possibility, we need to check that they have indeed been nominated by the branch they claim to be from.

I have my doubts. I noticed a couple of months ago that for some reason the most active and outspoken of the Militants had transferred to a 'new' branch that sent its maximum of five delegates. So I told Peter that I want to know the number of members in each of the T & G branches affiliated to Knowsley North.

If all else fails, that's what we'll catch them on. I'm sure, for instance, that the 6/612 branch does not have enough members actually living in my constituency to entitle it to its five delegates. Since a trade union branch can send delegates to my constituency management committee on the basis of one delegate for every 100 members or part thereof that *live* – and that's the operative word – in Knowsley North, I shall insist that this 6/612 branch proves that it has 401 members living on my patch. I don't believe it has. Nor, I suspect, have some of the others.

There's another factor, too. For the delegates to be validly nominated the union has to pay a subscription for each delegate. Instead of paying in £5 each time for each delegate, as almost all other organisations do, the T & G pays a lump sum to cover all its delegates from all the branches. It hasn't paid enough, apparently. At the management meeting last week Peter Killeen announced that the T & G has only paid £110. That covers 22 delegates, so they'll have to lose at least a dozen. My job is to ensure that when it comes to deciding who is to be amongst the dozen it is the Militants who are discarded and not my supporters – but as that will be done by the regional office of the union I should be all right.

However, my colleagues at the conference did not think that I was all right. A rumour had gone round, started it seems by Barry Sheerman, the MP for Huddersfield and an old friend from LSE days, that I had been deselected on Sunday. Several of my parliamentary colleagues commiserated with me. It was annoying. It showed me how small a ripple the news had caused. It had curiosity value, no more: a case of 'tut tut' and pass on.

Tuesday 1st October 1985

There can never have been a speech like it. I've certainly never heard one, nor expect to ever again. It was electrifying. When he got to the part about the 'grotesque spectacle of a Labour Council, a *Labour* Council, hiring taxis to scuttle round the city handing out redundancy notices to its own workers', it was as if a bomb had exploded.

The conference floor erupted. And that bastard Heffer, the prima donna to outdo all prima donnas, got up and lumbered off the platform and out of the hall. The shit. The absolute shit. And that's just what I called him: the language from my parliamentary colleagues standing around me was still more colourful and apt. He'd been waiting for the opportunity, of course. I was watching him throughout the speech. He sat aloof, at the front of the stage just to the left of Neil, disdainful right from the very beginning. He didn't laugh, as everyone else did, at Neil's comparison of Tebbitt and Whitelaw to arsenic and old lace, and I never once saw him applaud.

I was afraid for Neil, worried that he would think the booing and the jeering was directed against him instead of against Heffer, as most of it was. I was afraid that he would not be able to continue his speech, and that if he did sit down he would be defeated, the conference would disintegrate, and the party would be destroyed. He looked so small and vulnerable a figure on that large red and grey platform in that massive hall.

But he didn't. He stood his ground. He waited for the noise to subside and went on. It was fantastic. I felt immense relief. It was as if his words had lanced a great boil that had been gathering and festering in my chest all summer.

He said what I had wanted to say. He told the truth. He led, courageously, from the front.

I stood and clapped and cheered, urging some of my more reluctant or inhibited parliamentary colleagues to do likewise. My voice was hoarse and my hands sore by the time I went looking for Jan.

I couldn't find her. The foyer and the bars were crammed with groups of excited and arguing delegates, television cameras and lights and radio reporters pushing their microphones and tape recorders under the nose of anyone who would comment. I did an interview for Kent Barker, a BBC radio reporter for *The World at One*, hardly able to hear my own voice for the noise around me. I made instant comments for David Utting of the Liverpool *Daily Post* and Andy Grice of the *Liverpool Echo*, before being whisked off by James Hogan, a BBC TV producer, to do a live television interview with Robin Day.

I sat next to Robin in the sun on the veranda of the Bournemouth conference centre, overlooking the sea. There was a clear blue sky. While we waited to be slotted into the programme, the Militants arrived. As I left the conference hall I'd seen Terry Fields, the Militant supporter MP for Liverpool Broadgreen, summon Eddie Loyden, the member for Liverpool Garston, out of the MPs' enclosure. They were gathering their forces. Now they were all here.

Fields, Loyden, Hatton and Mulhearn, and Hamilton, the nominal leader of Liverpool City Council, and dozens of those Militant youths with badges plastered all over their donkey coats and pints of beer in their hands, stood just the other side of the cameras, almost level with the camera lens – only a couple of yards away from me. They leered, as their ilk do in Knowsley.

Robin beckoned the floor manager over and urged him to get a move on before they overran the place. The atmosphere was tense and threatening. Hatton was to be interviewed after me, Robin explained, and he came on his own initiative and stood directly behind me. I don't know if they really thought that they were frightening me, but they weren't. I said what I've been looking for an occasion to say all these long summer months. I couldn't wait to say it.

As I pushed through the mob after the interview, you could almost touch their anger towards me, and particularly towards Neil. I was still high enough on Neil's rhetoric to stride up to the quiet whispering group of John Prescott, the shadow Employment Minister and MP for Hull East, Jack Straw, the MP for Blackburn, and Bob Wareing, the member for Liverpool, West Derby. They were leaning against the wall in the grey corridor.

'I hope,' I said, marching up to them and interrupting, 'you're all going to back him up now. He deserves our support.'

Jack and Bob said nothing. Bob looked at John Prescot.

'It all depends on whether you want all-out war or not,' John said, critically.

'All-out war? What d'you mean? We've already got all-out war. It's just that the good guys have started fighting back,' I said.

'I'm not so sure,' he said.

His caution is disturbing, because he's a smart political operator and a natural supporter of Neil. If people like him don't publicly back Neil up to the hilt now then we shall lose the party to the Militants and the election to the Alliance. I know there's no place in the middle. You just get run down by both sides if you stand there.

I turned to Bob Wareing. 'And as for you,' I said, deliberately aggressive, 'you've got to support Neil on this.'

'Who, me?' he asked, incredulous.

'Yes, you. If you and the rest had taken a strong stand against them we wouldn't be in this mess.' I stalked away. He ran after me. He plucked my sleeve.

'Listen,' he said. I stopped and turned to face him. 'I don't support them. I've fought them as much as anyone.'

'You could have fooled me,' I retorted. 'I suppose you were really opposing them when you marched alongside them on their demos, were you, Bob?' I added, sarcastically. I made to move away.

'Listen,' he said. He grabbed my arm again.

'I can't be bothered, Bob,' I said. I shook my arm free. I strode off.

He's not a bad bloke, Bob Wareing. In fact he's a decent sort. I suppose that's why I was so angry: you expect more from people like him.

The Militants are very powerful in his constituency, as indeed they are in all the Liverpool seats, and on much of Merseyside. You can see why any Labour MP has to be seen at Labour Party functions organised by Militant, but nevertheless the MP's presence lends them the credibility and respectability that is so crucial to their success.

I can remember when we were urging Heffer to stand for the deputy leadership of the party against Denis Healey and Tony Benn. We didn't actually want to support him, although he thought we did. We just wanted someone on whom we could waste our votes, instead of being forced to vote for Benn. (Neil, incidentally, had already quite properly refused our entreaties to be our candidate.) Heffer swallowed our flattery, as we always knew he would. Yes, he said, he would stand. Then his local party said that he couldn't, so he chickened out. That was bad enough, especially as we had spent a considerable amount of time organising and preparing his campaign. But even then he couldn't relinquish the limelight. At the meeting that had been called to decide upon his replacement he said that he wouldn't be standing as a candidate but that he had written a good speech that he would have made had he been announcing his candidature and could he read it to us. And he did. Or at least he began to. He sat at the head of the green leather-topped desk in a committee room of Westminster Hall, and read from his typescript. Through the lead-lined windows behind him the London traffic could be seen rushing down the Embankment. I looked at the two ex-Cabinet Ministers, John Silkin, the MP for Lewisham, Stan Orme, the MP for Salford East, and all the rest. Like me they were embarrassed. I nudged Stan's knee. 'Stop him,' I whispered. Stan pretended not to have heard. John Silkin winked at me. I looked imploringly at my friend and fellow Brummie, Jeff Rooker, the MP for Birmingham Perry Barr, but he avoided my eyes. 'This is ridiculous,' I whispered again. I couldn't believe that they were all prepared to sit there and listen to him.

Finally, after he had read several pages with what looked like a dozen to follow, I intervened to stop him.

'What are you reading this out for, Eric?' I asked innocently, as if I had not understood his reason.

'Well, I thought you'd like to hear what I would have said. It's very good.' He smiled, looking at the faces surrounding him. 'Even if I do say so myself.' He pushed the bridge of his glasses up his nose with the forefinger of his right hand.

'Are you standing, Eric?' I demanded. The others looked uncomfortable. John Silkin stared out of the window. Stan Orme suddenly found his finger nails to be inordinately interesting. Jeff bit his bottom lip.

'No . . .'

'Well, can we get on and decide who is? I've got another meeting to go to,' I lied. It was brutal but he deserved it. He should not have had the vanity to subject us to his speech and so run the risk of being humiliated. But I don't think he even noticed what had happened. He probably thought we did have another meeting to attend. I'm not sure now, but I think I recall him saying that he would have copies made and would circulate them. I wonder if he did? Have them circulated, I mean. I must ask John Silkin, he'll remember.

Today, at the Conference, Heffer was still playing to the gallery. It strikes me that he has never got over the fact that he wasn't elected to the leadership of the party in 1983. He thinks, God help us, that he *should* be the leader. I can still remember him complaining at lunch in the sunlit dining-room of the Imperial Hotel in Blackpool when Neil was first elected to the NEC and saying that it had taken him ten years and Neil only a couple. He resented that.

Back in the foyer I eventually found Jan. The excitement was intense and pervasive. Like all those on 'our' side, she couldn't stop smiling. We had to wrench ourselves away to go to a fringe meeting. We walked back up the hill telling the long lines of Militant newspaper sellers to 'stuff it' as they called out their anti-Labour slogans. They didn't like it. They were fine at shouting at you when they were in a group. They didn't have much to say for themselves when you stopped, as we repeatedly did, to ask 'And who are you shouting at?'

To think that before all this at lunchtime Michael Cockerell and his producer, Tom Barnicoat, and researcher did not seem to be bothered about whether or not they got back to the conference centre in time to hear Neil's speech.

We met them for lunch at The Crust in Bourne Avenue, The Square, to discuss the programme. Even then I was still reluctant and apprehensive about starting an all-out war on the Militants in my constituency, but all that has changed in the course of the day. Neil has drawn the battle lines. I know which side I'm on. I also know that, despite my colleagues' repeated comment that 'this'll be good for you', it won't be. What Neil has done will mean that good Labour voters will rally to him and to common sense in the rest of the country but that on Merseyside, because it's different, they'll rally to Militant.

Back to lunch. I agreed to co-operate with them on the film. I told them the situation, briefly. They seemed incredulous, naturally. It's difficult to convince ordinary decent people of the truth of some of the more murky aspects of Knowsley politics that cannot be mentioned even here. They were also politically uninformed, at least on the constitution and workings of the Labour party. So I had to give a lecture on how the General Management Committee is made up and how people become delegates before we could get to the real nitty gritty.

All the time Jan and I were watching the clock and eating little, anxious to be back in good time for that historic speech. Dinner was different. It was a riot. Bevins took Jan and me to the Pasta Joint, together with Jeff Rooker and his secretary, Janet. We usually have one dinner together at conference and they're normally boisterous and good fun. Because of our feelings about Neil's speech, tonight's was hilarious. We are all in good heart and high spirits. The good times are coming. A Labour Government now looks possible.

There is, however, a small private part of me that refuses to celebrate, that is keeping its distance from the festivities. It's telling me that I won't be a part of the celebration of the next Labour Government. It's a nasty feeling.

Wednesday 2nd October 1985

All I wanted to do was to sit quietly in the hotel lounge and watch the early evening television news. I was curious to see how they would report Neil's second conference speech, which was shorter but equally extraordinary and electrifying, this time demolishing Scargill.

I didn't get to see it. I had a fist fight instead.

Several of us were sitting in the hotel lounge waiting for the news to begin: three young trade union delegates, Jack Pimblett, the full-time agent for Gordon Oakes, the MP for Widnes, and his wife. Jan hadn't finished drying her hair.

As the news programme began, a youth who had been making himself conspicuous in the hotel all week appeared and strutted in the open doorway. He began talking. One of his seated mates put a forefinger to his lips and motioned him to be quiet.

Neil appeared on the screen.

'Bollocks,' the man in the doorway exclaimed. I winced, expecting Jack Pimblett to reprimand him. Jack is the age my stepfather would have been had he lived and much the same type, and he would, I thought, be offended by the use of such language in front of his wife. The youth, hands thrust deep into the trouser pockets of his smart suit, his shoulders swaying as he chewed gum, seemed oblivious to such sensibilities. He started to chatter.

'Come on pal,' I said, eventually. 'We're trying to listen.'

'Say please,' he sneered. 'Say please. Weren't you brought up to say please?'

I should have hit him then, but I restrained my anger. 'Don't patronise me,' I said as quietly and as calmly as I could.

'Why?' he jeered. He swung his shoulder, his hands still in his pockets. 'You wanna fucking make something of it?'

He was calling me out, just as we used to do all those long years ago when I was a kid on the slum streets of Birmingham. I was sure he was about to hit me. There was no way that I could back down, so I hit him first. Just a left.

He went backwards so fast that, unfortunately, he put an elbow through a window.

I pulled him back by the throat, about to hit him again, but the fight, as they say, had gone out of him. Besides which, his mates were now restraining me. For a moment I thought that I was going to have to take them all on, but, like all his big-mouthed bullying sort, he couldn't cope with having his bluff called. He started whining.

'I'm going to tell the manager. I'm going to tell the police.' He walked toward the phone.

'Tell who you like,' I said. I turned back to watch the news. I was irritated – I had ripped and lost a button off the sleeve of a favourite shirt, which was fairly new. Jan would be annoyed.

'I shouldn't tell anyone if I was you,' Jack Pimblett said to the youth. 'You've no right to use offensive language like that in front of a lady.' So I was right: he had been upset and offended. 'If I hadn't got diabetes I'd have told you myself.' His wife added her support. 'You've no right to speak like that,' she said.

The youth brought the manager, at whom I winked conspiratorily and reassuringly. I'll pay for the window, I whispered to him without my assailant hearing. The youth phoned the police.

Jan was mortified when I told her what had happened. Not at what I'd done, but because she'd missed it.

Before we left for the *Daily Mirror* party some twenty minutes later I saw the manager again privately. I apologised for having caused a commotion in his hotel, and said that I would pay for the repair of the window – though I said the other fella, by rights, ought to pay half. No matter. Whoever's fault it was it certainly wasn't the hotel manager's and so I wanted him to be reassured.

'He's had it coming to him all week,' he said. He seemed delighted, in spite of the broken window.

On the way out of the hotel I also made a sort of apology to my protagonist, who was standing outside waiting for the police to arrive. 'I'm sorry for hitting you,' I said. 'But you can't go around talking to people like that and expect to get away with it.'

'I've rung the police,' he said. 'They're coming any minute. You'd better wait for them.'

We left.

I wasn't really worried about the justice of my case or about what I had done. I felt totally confident not only that I'd done the right thing, but that I had no alternative and that I would do it again. But I was concerned about the fuss that there might be, although Jan wasn't. She was adamant that I couldn't have done anything else, and that she wouldn't have wanted me to. She was great. But then she always is.

We walked arm in arm along the seafront to the Royal Bath Hotel, treading on crumpled and soiled Militant leaflets, as if we were a young courting couple without a care in the world.

Without telling me, Jan told Maggie Ashton what had happened, and she of course told her husband Joe, the MP for Bassetlaw and *Daily Star* columnist.

'Is that right?' Joe asked, interrupting my conversation with Robert Maxwell's daughter, Ghislane. We were standing in the dining-room of the Royal Bath at the party given by the *Mirror*. 'What your missus said? You put a Militant through a window?'

'Christ, Joe,' I said. 'She's not supposed to tell anyone.' I was surprised. We hadn't discussed it but I hadn't expected Jan to repeat the story, not even to good friends like the Ashtons.

'Why?' he said. 'That'll do you no harm. Do you a power of good, that. Want me to tell the press? That's the way to treat them.' He seemed as pleased as if he'd done it himself.

No, I said. I didn't want him to tell the press.

'You're wrong,' he said. 'Believe me.'

I actually agreed with his judgement, but recoiled from the way it might be portrayed. I didn't really want to be pictured as a brawler. I wasn't; it was just that I had been provoked and had responded in the way that my boxer grandfather had taught me.

'Well done,' said Don Concannon, the six-foot-four former miner and guardsman and now MP for Mansfield. His massive hand gripped my shoulder. 'Don't stand any bloody nonsense. Hit the buggers.'

I realised I was going to have trouble keeping it out of the papers.

All the time that this was going on I was eliciting the help of Muriel Turner, the assistant general secretary of ASTMS, and Clive Jenkins, the general secretary, in finding out about the three new apparently Militant-inspired delegates who had appeared from their union. Muriel was great. She'll help. I knew she would.

Clive was still high on Neil's speeches. In fact, they both were, and so were we all. During the speech this morning, Clive actually left his seat in the section right in front of the MPs' corral and strode up and down the gangway behind the last row of his delegates, muttering and clapping. It was as if he had undertaken the role of cheerleader, but he wasn't needed.

'Well, I wasn't telling lies,' Neil had responded to a heckler who asked what he'd been doing during the strike. He hadn't and he wasn't now. He said that he wasn't going to introduce retrospective legislation to help the miners, or anyone else. He was going to insist on the sanctity of the rule of law.

It was good heady stuff. The review of the cases of the jailed miners would be carried out by the normal judicial procedures, influence would be used to get reinstated by the National Coal Board those dismissed but innocent of any crime. But that was it. There will be no more.

'It would be dishonest,' he said, 'for the party to give an undertaking that somehow people could come into conflict with the common law, the civil law, or the criminal law, and that the cavalry, in the form of a future Labour Government, will pick up the tab. That will not happen,' he shouted above the uproar, 'and anyone who said that it would,' he continued, barely making himself heard above the pandemonium, and straining that vulnerable voice, 'would not convince the British people.'

It was a shorter speech than the seventy-minute one he made yesterday, but it was equally emotional, powerful and, above all, unequivocal. Whatever else they may say, there can be no doubt about where Neil Kinnock and the Labour party stand. And on this occasion, it is upon the firm rock of adherence to the law and the telling of the truth. The boy's got class.

There can be few things more invigorating, refreshing and inspiring than a political leader telling an unpalatable but necessary truth. As I said on *The World at One*, there is a new phenomenon in British politics. We have the leader of a major political party who tells the truth, who knows the difference between right and wrong and says so. It's wonderful.

I wondered if the brief conversation that I had with Neil at the reception last night for visitors from overseas had influenced his speech. Jan had learned from a good source that Neil was being advised to tone down his attack on Scargill. MPs, he was told, are worried, but he had not been given the names of the faint hearts. It made me mad. None of the colleagues that I respect, and that I know Neil respects, took that view. They aren't political cowards, and they know that there is no going back now. Scargill has to be hammered. He's had it coming to him. It's Neil's turn to be on top politically. Some things now have to be said, loud and clear.

Ignoring the television cameras and the lights I pushed through the throng of dignitaries to Neil. I wouldn't normally have done that, but this was important. In spite of my obvious rudeness in intruding he greeted me warmly.

'Don't listen to the wimps about tomorrow,' I said. 'You know what the truth is, tell it. You can't go wrong if you tell the truth.'

'I know,' he replied confidently. He winked. He knew what I meant.

'Just follow your instincts. That's all we ask.'

'I will,' he said. 'Don't worry.' He gripped my shoulder hard.

And he did. It was great. He said all the things that I've wanted to hear him say all summer. At last we're back to knowing the difference between right and wrong.

Just to make sure that the supportive message got home I'd repeated it to Glenys. She's no problem. She's tough. If only the two of them were left alone to make the decisions, allowed to follow their own instincts, instead of being constantly cautioned and reined back, we'd have no difficulties.

But perhaps that's just what I think. We're of the same age, from similar backgrounds, with the same values and priorities. There are a lot of us in that generation who, like Neil and Glenys, owe all our 'life chances' to the post-war Labour Government.

During the speech, every MP was listening to what their leader said, unlike the 1983 conference when we had the sight of Austin Mitchell, MP for Great Grimsby, writing an article on Icelandic fishing, of all things, during Michael Foot's valedictory speech. But as in previous years, Tony Benn was conspicuously absent from the platform when Neil spoke. Today we also had the pantomime of Dennis Skinner doing everything possible to draw attention to himself. This time he stalked back and forth behind Neil, leaned over Doug Hoyle, the MP for Warrington North, or Tom Sawyer, the deputy general secretary of NUPE, to carry on a conversation in the front row. Then he sat down directly behind Neil and well within the TV camera line, a scowl on his face, sucking Imperial mints with Joan Maynard, the hard left MP for Sheffield Brightside, nicknamed 'Stalin's Granny'. What a pair.

I don't know why Dennis behaves like this, but he always does, at least in public. He doesn't like many of his colleagues, of course. Dennis is a terrible man in public, yet privately he's charming and full of humour, even against himself. Jan likes him a lot. Chris

Mullin, former editor of *Tribune*, once called him a 'ballerina'. It was his explanation of why Dennis sat black-macked and scowling at the back of the Pavilion in Brighton at the 1983 Tribune Rally, instead of being one of its stars on the platform as usual. Dennis, he said, had refused to appear because he'd been asked last. 'You know Dennis,' Mullin said. 'He's a proper ballerina.' I think he meant prima donna.

With prima donnas such as these, it's a wonder that we ever get anywhere with the public. Incidentally, it also explains why Eric – puffed up with self-importance – Heffer has to go to such lengths to compete with them.

But at least they're working class. The parlour socialists are much worse, probably because they feel the need to prove themselves. I love the way they so arrogantly claim to speak for the working class. For example, Harriet Harman, daughter of a consultant physician, niece of the Earl of Longford, and now MP for Peckham, berated Jeff Rooker and myself for not voting for Tony Benn in the deputy leadership contest. We'd betrayed socialism and the working class.

We both resented that, especially as it had come from someone with no experience of a father unemployed or on strike, of a mother using the rent money to buy food and the gas money to repair shoes, and, when the latter failed, of walking to school with cardboard in your soles. Unlike the parlour socialists, I don't need to prove my working-class credentials. I was born with them and in poverty. I certainly don't need to wear shabby clothes, live in a decrepit house and drive a rusty car, as some of them do, in order to prove that I'm a socialist. I've had all that. The difference was that for me it was real.

After the *Daily Mirror* party and before the Channel 4 reception, Tony Bevins told me there was a story going around that Ken Cure, a tough and no-nonsense Brummie and the AUEW member of the national executive, was going to put a motion to the NEC to expel Hatton. That sounded right. But why, I wonder, stop at Hatton? By the time I spoke to Ken others had obviously got to him too, including a very predatory-looking Germaine Greer. I know what he wants to do: he wants to put them all out, no messing. I merely wanted to know how he would do it. He wasn't sure; he was being urged to tread carefully.

That worries me. Not because I'm particularly anxious to see Hatton or anyone else expelled, though I am, but because it looks as if there is already some of the ultra-caution that, if allowed to predominate, could undo all the good that Neil's speech has achieved. Immediately after the speech the press were already asking: 'What's the next move? What happens next? Surely,' they keep enquiring, 'it doesn't stop with the speech?' I hope not, but some MPs are saying it will. It *can't*. If there is no attempt made to reclaim the Labour party in Liverpool from the Militants, then it would have been better if the speech had never been made. We shall all stand condemned, and Neil will look as if he is all words and no action.

That's the last thing he is, and it's the last thing that we can afford him to be accused of now. But people are already backing off. They're looking carefully to see which way things are moving before they commit themselves. They always do. That's why they survive and the Labour party loses.

My problem is that I feel inhibited in saying all this to him. I'm compromised by my constituency difficulties. I know that I would still be saying the same thing if I had no Militant problem: as Michael Crick's book *Militant* points out, I was one of those who constantly sought an audience with Michael Foot to urge him to take action against them well before the 1983 election. There were many times when we sat in the Shadow Cabinet room insisting that we would have no chance of winning the next election unless they were expelled, and in those days in Ormskirk I had a decent, sensible, and moderate management committee with only a couple of Militants. Nevertheless, even then, it was the activities of the Militants that preoccupied the electors when I was on the doorsteps.

However, my colleagues don't necessarily remember that I suspect they see me, as having a vested interest, at best, or, at worst, as a whinger. Whatever their view I feel diffident about being as vigorous in expressing my view and in prosecuting it as I was before 1983.

I felt this when we again met Michael Cockerell and two of his colleagues. We sat on the veranda of a hotel overlooking the grey sea. A kestrel hovered perfectly stable at our eye-level over the cliffs in the strong wind. We made them admire its strength.

They are definite about going ahead with the film; in fact, they are very keen. They've even cleared the date for its showing: Sunday 27th October. They now want a list of people they should talk to, and the names of those who are against me as well as of those who are supporters. They want the history of the conflict, the reasons for it, and examples of how the battle is being fought out.

It's me that is on trial – at least that's what I feel. 'What's wrong with you that they should want to get rid of you? What have you done?' are the unintended implications of their questions. It's a horrible feeling to have to justify yourself constantly, especially when you know that the speech for the defence will be broadcast and its veracity picked over by millions of strangers, not all of whom will start out as sympathetic or even neutral.

Still, it has to be done. Why, then am I on trial? There are several reasons. The first is that I have my critics, as I've said. There are those who do not like me and never have. Yet even including the people who have opposed me since I abstained in the deputy leadership contest in 1981 they are still only a very small, if vindictive, minority. More important is that they have made common cause with the increased number of Militants that I inherited from Harold Wilson, in the neighbouring constituency which was partially absorbed to make Knowsley North. They are determined to be represented by a Militant MP, someone who will join hands with the neighbouring Militant supporter, Terry Fields.

They are also well organised. They travel together to the meetings in a bus supplied by the Kirkby Unemployed Centre, where a lot of them work, and then sit together in a large and intimidating block. As few of them have 'ordinary' jobs they are virtually full-time political organisers.

But there are other factors than the straightforward one of the Militant infiltration of the constituency party. The constituency borders Liverpool, which is significant because it means that we take our politics from Liverpool. Theirs is the lead that we're expected to follow. Because I won't do this, I am set apart, and I've become both an embarrassment and a target. The same has happened to Frank Field across the water in Birkenhead. You become even more of a target if virtually all your neighbouring parliamentary colleagues appear to be supporting the Liverpool Militants, as they do. To some extent or other, all the Liverpool Labour MPs have toed the Militant line on Liverpool. They have certainly been prepared to sponsor and sign the Commons motions, ask the right questions, give the appropriate and well-worn answers and attend all the necessary rallies and demonstrations. The fact that I do not do those things and that I make clear my opposition to Militant and to what it is doing to Liverpool in the name of the Labour party, sets me out as an important and legitimate target.

Just to complicate matters, straightforward political ambition also plays a part, especially in the case of Jim Lloyd, the leader of Knowsley Council. As I have already indicated, he has never made any secret of his parliamentary ambitions and of coveting my seat.

That's fine, insofar as he's entitled to entertain such ambitions for himself. What has happened in practice, however, is that for the last two years he has constantly undermined me in a fashion that is only open to the leader of a council. It's no coincidence, I'm sure, that most of the councillors representing my constituency who oppose me have Council chairmanships or vice-chairmanships given to them by Jim Lloyd. Nor does it seem to be a coincidence that – with one exception – the councillors on my management committee who support me do not, as I write this, have jobs in the Labour group, even though they are clearly some of the most long-serving and able councillors.

I can't compete with that. I have no patronage at my disposal. I can't dish out jobs that carry thousands of pounds in posts of special responsibility and experience; neither can I compete with the special relationship that Jim Lloyd has with Militant. He's very friendly with Derek Hatton who, of course, works for Knowsley Council on very favourable terms. His right-hand man on the Council, chairman of committees and Chief Whip, is the now notorious Tony Beyga, Hatton's friend and holiday companion. When Beyga was convicted of failing to disclose an interest when his wife's job was involved in Council discussions, he was represented by Keva Coombes, who also represents Hatton, and who is himself a contender, which only makes the mosaic of Knowsley and Merseyside politics more fascinating.

Jim Lloyd's flirtation with Militant, or at least with some of its powerful personalities and fellow travellers, will be to his detriment in the long term. I'm sure of that. But in the meantime it forms an alliance for bad that is difficult to counter. It is ominous that the Beyga family are now represented in force on the management committee and seem to have taken over the ward where Peter Fisher is the councillor due for re-election this year.

This all seemed too complicated, too bizarre, too far-fetched even, for Michael Cockerell and his colleagues. We left them with the promise that they could film me in the constituency next week. They

37

said that they would be spending the week in Liverpool speaking to the Militants and researching the film.

Jan and I didn't speak as we walked up one of Bournemouth's hills into what had now become a cruel wind. I was apprehensive. So, she confessed later, was she. We obviously had the same thoughts, the same misgivings. My anxiety was centred on how the film would present me, of course. Who wouldn't be anxious? But I was also concerned about the disruption and the aggravation that the actual filming would entail. If nothing else, it takes a lot of time, time that I really did not want to give, even if I could spare it.

Michael Cockerell didn't believe me when I said that many of my supporters wouldn't be prepared to speak to him, and certainly not on film. They would be afraid of the consequences. These might not amount to physical assault, though that was possible, but would definitely include a great deal of verbal abuse. They've had enough of that without courting more.

Thursday 3rd October 1985

'There'll be trouble if you don't,' Roland Boyes, the MP for Houghton and Washington, said. 'Take my advice. Pay for the bloody window, apologise and have done with it.'

Ann Clwyd, the recently elected MP for Ioan Evans' Cynon Valley, agreed.

We're staying at the same hotel. Looking his most serious, Roland called me over to their table as soon as he saw that I had finished breakfast.

Last night they were at Welsh Night (the dance for all the Welsh delegates, held in the Wessex Hotel) and apparently the loud-mouth that I punched was going round telling everyone what had happened and showing his bruised face as proof. He was threatening to tell the press if I did not agree to pay the full cost of the window and make a 'proper formal apology', as Roland put it.

'I've already apologised,' I said. 'I did so last night.'

'That doesn't count,' Roland countered. 'Not to him. He says he wants a proper one.'

'Bugger that.' And I meant it.

Ann poured more coffee into my cup.

I'd already told the manager, I said, that I'd pay for the window.

38

It had to be an expensive Victorian one didn't it? It couldn't have been just any old piece of glass. But no, I wouldn't apologise again.

'Then he'll tell the press,' Ann said. She looked anxious.

'Then he'll have to.'

'But that'll be bad for you,' Roland argued.

I didn't agree. As it happens, I don't want the story to be in the newspapers, but if it is then I'm not so sure that it will damage me. In fact, it'll probably do me some good. I'd be respected for it. I'm certainly not prepared to be blackmailed into a grovelling apology.

'Well, we all know our own constituencies best,' Roland replied in the way that MPs do when we believe that a colleague is making a dire mistake, but don't want to challenge his judgment openly. I'm grateful for their obvious concern and I appreciate their desire to help, but there's no more I can do. I feel justified in what I did by the provocation I've suffered. Jan agrees. Vehemently.

However, today wasn't a good day to have such things in the press. Nominations opened today. Each branch of the party and of the organisation affiliated to it would be meeting to decide which candidate to nominate for consideration by the management committee for the short-list for selection as the party candidate. I'm afraid to say I haven't done much to ensure that I get the maximum number of nominations. I haven't been constantly on the telephone urging people to attend branch meetings to vote for me, as I should have done. I can't decide whether my inaction is attributable to not caring any more, to laziness, or to a feeling that whatever I do will make no difference in this respect. The branches that will nominate me will and those that won't won't.

I know that it's not true though. I'm a professional politician: I know about organisation. That's what it's all about.

Then why didn't I do it? I suppose, I realise, that in some areas it would be impossible, certainly with the limited resources and time that I have at my disposal. But the real reason, I suspect, is arrogance. It's the feeling that I shouldn't need to. I've been the MP for nearly a dozen years and if after all that time and work I have to resort to pleading with people to turn up to ward meetings to vote for me then the game is really not worth the candle.

Unfortunately, I couldn't escape such considerations all day. I was constantly asked about 'your problem', even at the lunch given by Labour Friends of Israel at the Palace Court Hotel for Gad Ya'acobi, the Israeli Minister of Economics. I met him at the Tel Aviv flat of

Esther Herlitz, the ex-Israeli Ambassador to Denmark, when the Syrians were threatening to cut Israel in two and be in the city within hours during the Yom Kippur war.

'My problem' spoils things. Even such relaxed, pleasant and easy lunch companions as Bryan and Jill Gould and Colleen and Merlyn Rees, and the effervescent Gerald Kaufman, couldn't remove the cloud that was looming. It seemed strange to be sitting in the hotel in such company, remembering that I worked in its kitchens for an idyllic summer before my A-levels. Those, strangely, seem happier days. But then they were carefree and filled with promise.

We drove home up the M3 in the rain. Perhaps it was tiredness – or more likely the exhaustion of exhilaration – but we both seemed to be in a sombre mood and, uncharacteristically, spoke very little.

Southern England is undoubtedly beautiful, but whilst acknowledging and appreciating it, I also resent it. I suppose, I can't help but compare it both to where I come from in the slums of the back streets of Birmingham, and to the deprived and neglected areas that I now represent like Cantril Farm – or Stockbridge Village, to give it the name that Heseltine bequeathed it when selling it off to a Trust after the Toxteth riot. The south is so obviously affluent – its well-kept houses, its ordered and well-stocked gardens, the expensive quiet cars. As one of my constituents once said, the people seem to be permanently on holiday, protected from the sharp edge of life.

The Conference already seems far away. I'm not sure what its long-term consequences will be, but it ought at least to have established Neil as a leader. Those speeches must also have laid to rest any lingering doubts that people may have had about either his depth or his courage. He has both. I have always known that he had both. I've been surprised when other people, even some of our colleagues, have questioned whether or not he possesses these qualities. Now there can be no doubt.

Thinking about his speeches reminds me of his first major speech as leader at the 1983 conference. I'm sure I saw tears in the eyes of the former Home Office Minister, Shirley Summerskill, standing behind him on the platform. Jim Callaghan, next to me at the standing ovation, said, 'It's a good conference speech. The best for years. The trouble starts afterwards.'

At the time I thought him superior, playing the 'I've seen it all before' role that elder statesmen so frequently affect. But he was right.

Tony Benn was absent from the platform again, when Neil and Glenys were together on the platform. Dennis Skinner was there. And then, as now, he was scowling, pulling faces and drawing attention to himself by striding around the platform behind Neil and Glenys, wanting everyone to see that he disapproved. Some things don't change.

We conspired a great deal in those days. Jack Straw called a secret meeting that turned out to be hilarious. In great and conspiratorial secrecy, Jack convened a meeting of like-minded colleagues in the Tribune Group in order to discuss the state of candidates for the Shadow Cabinet elections that would take place, as they do every year, when the House met after all the Party conferences had finished. We met, however, in the ballroom of the Salisbury Hotel – in full view of everyone, as our table was on the stage! The first thing that Jack asked for, apart from total secrecy, was £3 each towards the cost of hiring the room.

Besides Jack and myself, Robin Cook, dear departed Ioan Evans, Kevin McNamara, John Prescott, Bob Hughes, Stan Orme and Gordon Brown were there. John Prescott said that there was no way that a cabal like that could be kept secret and was against the meeting. He had a point. Bob Hughes had already blown our cover by talking about the meeting to me in front of Jeff Rooker, who had stupidly been excluded. Alf Dubs had invited Frank Dobson, who was not a member of Tribune, and Jack Straw had invited both Harriet Harman and Andrew Bennett when the former was a member of Tribune and the hard-left Campaign Group and the latter had left Tribune for the Campaign Group. It was a farce. We decided that we shouldn't meet again.

That was the Conference when, during one morning session, I sat next to John Silkin. He nudged me with his elbow and indicated a newspaper paragraph saying that Cecil Parkinson's secretary was having his baby. I shrugged. I didn't believe it. Anyway, I remember thinking, it's of no concern to anyone else.

It was at the same conference that I sat next to Jim Callaghan at the beginning of the debate on defence. Great efforts had been made, not least by his former parliamentary private secretaries, Jack Cunningham and Roger Stott, the MP for Westhoughton, to persuade him not to participate and so not disturb the delicate unity that was developing on the issue.

'I shan't speak unless I'm provoked,' he told me. Then he added, 'But I bet you that Moss Evans [the then general secretary of the T & G and a leading unilaterist] won't go into negotiations with a no-strike clause.' In fact, of course, he was provoked by the fiery speech from Gavin Strang, the MP for Edinburgh East, who accused Callaghan of having contributed to our election defeat by the speech on defence he made in Cardiff during the campaign.

Callaghan confided to me that he'd enjoyed the BBC TV film that had been made about me by Clive Sydall for *Midweek* when I was first elected and in which I said yes, I did want to be Prime Minister. Unfortunately I'd added, tongue in cheek, that it would take fifteen years. Callaghan's not too delicate reminder of it showed that it still rankled, even with an ex-Prime Minister.

He said, somewhat smugly, 'We thought it so open, so honest, so straightforward.' He meant stupid and naive. 'I shall have to watch out for him,' I said to Audrey. Then, no doubt as a consolation, he told me how well I had done on Home Office affairs, the police, human rights and prisons, but advised me that I must broaden my base. Someone from behind, I think it was David Winnick, the MP for Walsall North, leaned over our shoulders and asked about my book, *The Ceremony of Innocence*, that was then on sale at the Conference bookshop. Philip Whitehead, who had just lost his seat in Derby, had described it in that day's *Fabian Conference News* as a 'tough tale about the British police state we might live to see, if we don't curb it first. Pick it up,' he had written, 'at the Labour bookstall.' That's what friends are for.

'What book's that?' Jim Callaghan asked.

'A novel,' I answered.

'A novel?' he snorted. 'Well, you'll never become Prime Minister now.'

I walked round the garden when we got home. There's a lot to do. The wallflowers will need to be planted out this weekend. This year Jan has decided to have single colours instead of the variegated ones that we and everyone else normally have. My wife has to be different. She's chosen white and pink. I've sown the seeds in three long rows between the raspberries and the blackcurrant bushes. The only trouble is that I can't remember which row is which colour. I haven't told Jan yet.

Then the *Star* rang. They'd heard about the fight at the hotel. 'No comment.'

'We understand that you put a Militant through the window . . .'

'I'm sorry, I have no comment.' I put the phone down. That, I presumed, would be it, but not a bit of it. An hour later and there was this very young, very public school, very apologetic and very wet young man on the doorstep. 'Please, Mr Kilroy-Silk,' he said. I was firm but polite.

'No comment.'

Friday 4th October 1985

Well, the *Star* carried the story all right. It's the main item in the Peter Tory column. It dominates the whole page, most of which is devoted to a picture of me when I was younger. The headline reads: 'Smashing Kilroy(Silk) was Here'. The subtitle says: 'A Touch of Glass Warfare at the Hotel.'

It wasn't bad. It was written sympathetically, and seemed to be on my side.

I was right, too: it was the main topic of conversation in each of my four surgeries this evening in Knowsley. 'I hope you gave him a belting', 'That's the way to treat 'em', 'I didn't think you'd got it in you', 'Well done, lad', were but a few of the comments of my constituents, the last spoken with an extended arm and the firm shake of a gnarled hand in The Harvester public house in Cantril Farm. The comments were repeated afterwards in the Prescot Labour Club. People smiled knowingly at me. I must have been given half a dozen copies of the cutting from the *Star* by my amused constituents. One very elderly lady told me of her need for help to buy blankets and sheets and then said, 'Hang on love. I've got something for you.' She rummaged in her bag and then her purse and eventually extracted a piece of soiled newspaper folded to the size of a postage stamp, which she then proceeded to open out. I pretended that I'd not seen it before.

It's good to have your judgment proved right, and it's even better to receive such a response. Jan, who shared my estimation of the likely consequences if the incident were to be publicised, will be pleased, especially as I'd blamed her for accidentally leaking the story.

At least the incident enlivened my surgeries. There were lots of people waiting to see me at each of the four locations where I hold my regular Friday surgeries, though there are always more at the Municipal Buildings in Kirkby than anywhere else. Housing, as always, was the major problem. But there was also a case of alleged police ill-treatment, several claims for social security payments, confusion over housing benefit, demands for a garden fence to be erected, a house to be fumigated, a troublesome neighbour removed, a son to be released from prison on compassionate grounds, and someone with a dispute with their employer over their pension rights.

Though varied, the requests are fairly routine. Most will be dealt with by letter. Sarah will be busy on Monday, as always. So will my quiet but diligent researcher, Noni Stacey. I'm lucky to have them working for me. They both take a personal and detailed interest in my constituents' problems and in sorting them out. A couple of the complaints will require me to have a private word with the appropriate minister as well. Ironically, the area where we have direct control, housing, will be the one where the fewest problems will be satisfactorily resolved.

Before leaving for the constituency this morning I'd rang the convenor at the BICC complex in Prescot, Joe Roby, and the managing director, Harry Hunter. I asked if Michael Cockerell and the BBC TV film crew could accompany me on a visit on Tuesday. No problem. They're happy to help. It's good to have friends.

Mind you, I have done a great deal for them. They've had several closures and redundancies since they came into the constituency in 1983. On each occasion I'd asked questions in the House, sought an emergency debate and met the senior management. This time I'd not only taken the problem direct to the Prime Minister, after seeing the chairman, Sir William Barlow, but also managed to extract extra concessions for the redundant workers from the company.

Incidentally, it was on the last occasion that I saw the Prime Minister about a BICC closure that I managed to trap her into agreeing to see twenty-five unemployed young people from Knowsley at No. 10.

We had tea together in her room at the House of Commons. She poured. We sat opposite each other on matching armchairs with a floral print in a corner of the large bright L-shaped room dominated by the massive polished table around which the Cabinet sits.

Although bright sunlight filtered through the tall stained-glass window high above where we sat near the stone fireplace, the large brass table lamps either side of us were lit. Dennis Skinner, who wanders round the Palace switching on lights to help the miners, would have been pleased.

She was well-briefed about the proposed factory closure and about the problems of Kirkby, Knowsley, Prescot and Merseyside, just as she had been when I had previously seen her in Downing Street about the closure of the kitchen furniture manufacturers, Hygena, in Kirkby, and here in this room over the closure of the Courtaulds factory in Aintree and then BICC Industries, Prescot. And, as on those occasions, it was difficult to get a word in. I managed to. The Industry Ministers who'd sat with us, first Keith Joseph, then Ken Baker and now John Butcher, never did – or rather they did, but she never let them finish a sentence. She treated them as if they were irrelevant.

She refused to stop the closure or avert the redundancies. I only just prevented her from giving me a lecture on the virtues of competition. She did, however, agree to ensure that both the Department of Industry and the Department of the Environment would do everything possible to help the company to re-train and re-locate those who were to be made redundant. She also promised that the Government would try to attract new-technology industries to Knowsley.

As at our previous meeting, I used this occasion to talk about the scale of unemployment in Knowsley: of how male unemployment in my own constituency had been 32 per cent when the 1981 census was taken and that since then we had lost over 10,000 jobs. In her constituency of Finchley the rate of unemployment was seven per cent. I pointed out that there were blocks of flats in Kirkby and Cantril Farm where not a single person was in work and of how unemployment was demoralising whole communities. She nodded sympathetically, especially when I pointed out that food shops like Fine Fare were now closing through lack of trade.

'Yes,' she said, shaking her head. 'Of course the trouble with your constituents is that they're not self-starters, are they? They don't start up their own businesses. They've no entrepreneurial spirit. They've got no get-up-and-go.'

I was flabbergasted. 'But that's ridiculous. You don't understand,' I began.

'There must be plenty of scope for one-man businesses. Why don't they go round mending electric kettles and dish-washers? I can never get my electric kettle repaired.'

I couldn't believe it, but she was serious. 'You've got no idea of what you're talking about,' I said. 'You've no conception of the depth and scale of the problem. Why don't you come and see? Meet the people . . .'

'Oh I'd love to,' she said in her gravelly voice. 'But Robert, you know the problem. There'd be demonstrations. Noise.' She examined the large green stone of the ring on a finger of her left hand. It matched the immaculate green two-piece suit. 'I wouldn't be able to hear what they had to say.'

'Meet them here,' I said quickly.

She hesitated. She glanced at her private secretary, Tim Fletcher.

'I'll organise it,' I said, quickly again. I could sense a coup. 'I'll book a room here. I'll bring a coach load. You'll have to pay for the coach though,' I said, smiling.

'All right,' she said looking at Tim. 'We'll have to get the money from charity.'

I could hardly believe it. 'I'll ring you and fix the details,' I said quickly to Tim. I wanted to get off the subject before she realised what she had committed herself to and changed her mind. 'I'll choose the kids,' I added as an afterthought, just in case they decided to seek the help of the local Conservative Association.

'Of course.'

In fact, I didn't select them. I asked the members of the party in each of the four main parts of the constituency to do that under the general supervision of Geoff Kneale. I told them to be sure to include members of the party and the sons and daughters of party members. It was, after all, probably the only chance they would ever get to see the inside of Number 10. The only stipulations I laid down were that they should be aged between sixteen and twenty-two, that there should be a more or less equal number of each sex, that they should be unemployed and that the local churches and youth clubs should be invited to nominate representatives. Several of the most articulate and outspoken came, in fact, from the Church of England's youth club in Kirkby.

Except for a few of those that I already knew as relatives of party members I did not meet the 'kids' until they arrived in the coach of a firm owned by a party member at the entrance of the House of

Commons in March. They were met by Neil Kinnock – of course – hordes of television and radio cameras and press men and torrential rain. In fact it had been difficult to get hold of any of them for the last couple of days. I had been virtually acting as their press agent. I had already arranged for four to stay for two nights in a London hotel as the guests of BBC TV *Breakfast Time*, on which they appeared the morning before and the morning after meeting the Prime Minister. Another two came down for TV am, stayed in a hotel for one night, ordered champagne, didn't like it, sent it back and asked for beer. All the rest were filming with ITN, Canadian TV, German TV and other radio and television programmes to set the scene of their homes and their towns. When my local Granada TV finally woke up to what was happening and asked me for a couple to interview there were none left.

When the coach drew up at Downing Street in the afternoon I thought it was going to be a disaster. They'd been quiet and respectful when listening to and asking questions of Neil in a committee room in the House. They had even been relatively subdued during the lunch with Ken Livingstone arranged by Sarah at County Hall. I called them together round a large table, told them that they mustn't be shy or intimidated, that they must all speak about their own experiences and to remember that they were also speaking for the other ten thousand unemployed that we'd left behind in Knowsley North. One of them was concerned to ensure that I would be accompanying them; another enquired if they would all have to ask questions. This wasn't very reassuring, but I need not have worried. They were superb. I was proud of them: they did a wonderful job for all the unemployed.

The Prime Minister met us on the first floor at the top of the wide stairs. She shook each one by the hand and ushered them towards a large table loaded with cake and tea, and then led us to the State dining room. She sat in the middle of the large oval table and I sat opposite her. The kids spread out either side of and behind me. They lit cigarettes. Ashtrays were summoned. The room quickly filled with smoke.

The Prime Minister began by welcoming us and then introduced her colleagues. To her left were Patrick Jenkin, the Secretary of State for the Environment, Peter Morrison, the Minister of State at the Department of Employment, Brian Nicholson, the chairman of the Management Services Commission, the Manager of the Job Centres in the North West, her private secretary and a vicar. Her press secretary, Bernard Ingham, lounged directly behind her. To her right were three industrialists, from Vauxhalls, Dewhurst's and Trust House Forte, and some careers advisers. However, she didn't get very far with the introductions before there was a loud crash on the table at the far end to my right.

'Never mind about that,' Rita Kneale, my agent's daughter, said aggressively. 'What about jobs? We've come here to talk about jobs.'

The Prime Minister looked at me in alarm. 'Are we going to do this properly?' she asked, fingering her necklace.

'Hold on a minute, Rita,' I said. 'Let the Prime Minister finish.'

When she'd finished I asked Philip Dunford, the oldest and the longest unemployed, to put the first question, as I had arranged with him that he should. It was the only thing I did arrange. Philip, sitting just behind me, spoke. The Prime Minister looked at me. 'I'm sorry,' she said, 'could you speak up?' She looked at me again, this time with a hint of helplessness in her eyes. Philip was, in fact, speaking very loudly. I could hear every word. 'I'm sorry,' she said again. 'I still can't hear.' She looked at me desperately. Then I realised. It wasn't that she couldn't hear. She couldn't understand. That really worried me. Philip's was by no means the broadest of their accents. I interpreted.

She told him and the others that they should move to other parts of the country in search of work, even go into lodgings. 'Why should we?' several called out.

'We did,' she said, looking at me.

'That's not the same . . .' I began to counter.

Rita interrupted. 'Don't you tell me about living in lodgings. I've done it all. I've lived in hostels and I've slept on the bare boards on the floor. I know all about it. Listen,' she said, leaning across the table and wagging her finger, 'I've even worked in Germany. And you know what I was doing? I was working in Germany making things for a British firm that exported them back here. Where's the sense in that then, eh?' she challenged.

They all began to speak. 'Hold on, kids,' I said. 'Let the Prime Minister answer.' I didn't want them to let her off the hook so easily. Patrick Jenkin rolled his eyes ceilingwards. A red patch began to creep up Mrs Thatcher's neck.

'Well . . .' she began. She was struggling.

48

'Mrs Thatcher,' the quiet and polite Helen Barlow intervened. 'My mother's a widow. I'm the only one at home. Why should I have to leave home to work somewhere else?'

The Prime Minister looked at me for help. I looked at Patrick Jenkin. He slowly covered his eyes with his right hand. Peter Morrison concentrated on examining the top of the table. Other kids started to ask questions.

'Hang on,' I insisted. 'I know the Prime Minister will want to answer. Give her a chance.'

And that's the way that it went. They murdered her. They realised that she did not know about and still less understand their problems. She was from a different world. It was that which made them angry and articulate. For example, she told them to start their own businesses.

'Oh, great,' one of them said. 'I get £22 a week. How am I supposed to start my own business on that?'

She could not attempt to answer most of their questions and those answers that she provided were inadequate. I have never seen her so much at a loss for words and so uncomfortable. Her neck was crimson when we left. Before we left I handed her the bill for the coach. I thought I ought to get it in quick before they decided the constituency should pay.

Mind you, the kids were not without wit. On the steps of Number 10 afterwards they gave an impromptu press conference to the assembled newsmen.

'But are there really no jobs on Merseyside?' a disbelieving *Daily Mail* man asked.

'Jobs on Merseyside?' one of the lads answered. 'Jobs on Merseyside are as plentiful as crap from a rocking horse.'

And so they are.

The propaganda value to the Labour Party of all this was enormous. The Tories acknowledged that. 'A disaster from start to finish,' Tom King, the Secretary of State for Employment, said to me in the Dining Room at the House a couple of days later. 'Who authorised it?' Patrick Jenkin and Peter Morrison, both of whom were present, were of the same view.

The Militants in Knowsley think otherwise – or some of them do. The chairman, Jim McGinley, has been criticising me for taking the kids to see the Prime Minister. He wants a resolution from his branch condemning me. Yet several of his supporters were the most aggressive in ensuring that their children were among the lucky twenty-five. One of them even went so far as to include not only her son but her still-at-school daughter, until I intervened to stop her. This time McGinley is unlucky.

Saturday 5th October 1985

The papers this morning reported the death of Harry Cowans. I was shocked and saddened. It seems to have happened suddenly, or at least I wasn't aware that he had been ill. But that would be nothing new. Very often it is only when a colleague that is not a part of your own close coterie of friends or associates returns after an illness that you realise that he's been missing. It's a powerful antidote to any notions of indispensability, as is the immediate talk of the prospects for the by-election when someone dies. I must confess that I have never got used to the latter. I've always found it a little distasteful, offensive even, although I know that it's only realistic and that no disrespect or offence is meant to those who have died. That the by-election seems to follow the death so quickly nowadays is a retrograde and unfeeling trend. But then I suppose these changes do no more than mirror those in the rest of society. We're becoming harder, less caring, I don't like it.

I didn't know Harry very well but we got on together and I liked and respected him. I always enjoyed the very special way that he savaged the Tories with a combination of sarcasm and wit, especially the latter, and a hint of condescension. He would tuck his thumb into that broad leather belt he always wore, lean his elbow on the dispatch box and then, in that fine Geordie accent, say to the minister when putting him right: 'Listen 'ere, bonny lad.' He'll be missed. There aren't many of his type left. The Tories could never get the better of him, but they loved him.

The *Mirror* also had the story of my fight. It was a page lead. This time the headline was: 'MP Knocked Me Through Window.' It was a reasonably accurate account of what had happened. And it still seems to be doing me no harm. A smiling stewardess on the British Airways shuttle home to Heathrow from Manchester handed me a copy saying that the picture didn't do me justice, and added, almost admiringly, 'Did you really hit him?'

Then it was home to the problems of a teenage daughter. Natasha

50

had been out all night, or nearly. She was due back from a party at eleven o'clock – at least, that is what she promised Jan. However, she and the three girlfriends who were staying the night, didn't get in until three-thirty: the car giving them a lift home had broken down! Hmm.

Jan waited up, fretting and phoning the police every half hour to see if there had been any accidents. Of course, I slept through this family crisis in Knowsley. It's great to have a beautiful and vivacious sixteen-year-old daughter, but it's also a great worry.

'Yes,' I promised Jan. 'I'll speak to her.'

'I mean it,' Jan insisted. 'Don't you let her charm you.'

She will, of course. She always does.

And Liverpool lost to QPR. That's terrible. I hate us losing to anyone, but especially to southern, and in particular London teams. They've no right to beat us, or any northern club. It's some consolation that we're still second in the League, but it's annoying that we didn't take advantage of Manchester United's draw with Luton to claw back a little of that ten point lead.

Sunday 6th October 1985

Dave Montgomery's *News of the World* story about Derek Hatton duly appeared today. 'The Ritzy Life of Dandy Derek' says that the 'red wrecker' as it calls him, leads a 'life of luxury'.

Apparently he wears Pierre Cardin suits and tailored shirts, has had two foreign holidays in the last year, dines at expensive restaurants, has bought his daughter a pony, and has a friendship with an attractive blonde, but none of this is really important. What *is* important is their allegations that apart from receiving £10,000 in expenses from Liverpool City Council he also receives £11,000 a year from Knowsley Council for 'just 17½ hours a week', and that he has two 'minders'. They also claim that the Council's Ford Granada made two round trips from Liverpool to the Labour Conference in Bournemouth so that he could attend a Variety Club party in Liverpool 'to mark pop singer Gerry Marsden's twenty-five years in showbiz'.

I don't think the Prime Minister could get away with all that. I don't know another Labour leader who would want to. After all, someone has to pay, and the poor, as always, will be picking up the bill.

Collecting the fallen beech and laurel leaves, piling them into large crackling clumps and then wheelbarrowing them to the compost heap, and sweating in the process, felt very satisfying. It was honest tiring work, and it seemed a far cry from the ritzy life of a Liverpool Militant.

My house *is* beautiful, and I love it. Mind you, it wasn't always like this. Whilst it wasn't exactly falling down when we bought it, it did need extensive repairs and modernisation. We've done a lot to it – or rather Jan has. She's been bricklayer, plasterer, electrician and decorator. I've helped, of course, but essentially it's her creation. Most importantly, it has all been done with our own money and time. No one else has ever contributed. Whatever I've got I've worked for and earned, like the good working-class lad that I am.

Working on some of the correspondence that Sarah left was also satisfying, especially as we seem to have solved a couple of problems and won a few cases that I've been doubtful about. One of them concerned a constituent who wrote asking for help with gaining entrance to Manchester University. He has three grade Bs at 'A' level but failed 'O' level English Language and so has not matriculated. He seemed to have been unfairly treated, especially as he had not been put in for the 16+ English examination by his school. The Joint Matriculation Board agreed, and we got him in.

I'm having far less success, however, in getting the husbands and boyfriends of five Liverpool women moved from prison in Glasgow to one in England so that it will be easier for their relations to visit. This will take some time but I don't think the women appreciate it. They know it's unfair on them and their children and expect this to be recognised and action taken immediately to rectify it. They don't yet realise how slow and cumbersome our bureaucracy is. Manifest injustice or not, it still has to go through the system.

Monday 7th October 1985

I don't believe it. Joe Roby and the shop stewards at the BICC factory in Prescot are so afraid that the Liverpool Militants will cause trouble at the site that they've decided not to be filmed with me by Cockerell and co after all.

I rang Joe from the Excelsior Hotel at Manchester Airport to finalise the time of our meeting tomorrow and to make sure of the arrangements for the TV crew. I could tell there was a problem the moment he answered the phone. He wouldn't talk. He asked me to ring him in five minutes in the office of the managing director, Harry Hunter.

'Have I caused you problems?' I asked Harry.

'I'm afraid you have, Robert,' he said apologetically. We got on well together. He was straightforward and he wouldn't mess me around.

'Do you want me to call it off?' I asked.

'Well . . .'

'We'll call it off,' I said, firmly. I had decided. It isn't worth insisting on going ahead with the visit if some of the stewards are unhappy about it.

'Well, I'd like . . .'

'Forget it, Harry,' I said. 'I don't want to embarrass you or anyone else. I can't be bothered.'

He seemed relieved. 'I think it best,' he said. 'It's not me. You know that, don't you? It's not the company. I've told them. You can come here whenever you like and if you want to bring television cameras that's fine by us.'

I know that to be true. I have an inkling of where the difficulty lies, but I didn't expect to have it confessed so readily. The stewards were apparently quite happy about the visit. There was no reason why they should not be; they've always welcomed me warmly in the past. Then one of them suggested that as the film is about my reselection, and as I'm being opposed by the Militants, they would have 'the Liverpool heavy mob at the gates'. That scared them. They panicked. They tried to get the company to call it off. The management refused. The stewards were told that if they wanted to cancel the visit they must tell me themselves, but I did it for them.

I'm livid. So that's the support and thanks you get. I've spent a great deal of time with those stewards and on that company's problems and when it comes to the crunch they're not prepared to stand up and be counted alongside me, even to the very limited extent of being in the background of a film.

The 'Liverpool heavy mob' would not have been at the gates. Or at least I don't think they would have been; you can never tell. But that doesn't matter. Much more important is that the style and the tenor of politics on Merseyside has now become such that sensible, moderate and decent Labour party members and supporters like Joe Roby and the shop stewards at B.I.C.C. can actually believe that they might be subjected to physical abuse and intimidation if they are seen to be associated with me. It's another good example of how and why the Militants have been so successful, both on Merseyside and in my constituency. They succeed by fear, physical as well as political intimidation. If these men won't stand up and be counted, even in the limited way that they've been asked to, then what hope is there for the rest of us?

When the news was conveyed to Michael Cockerell at the Adelphi Hotel in Liverpool at least it helped to reinforce what I had been saying to him about the political atmosphere on Merseyside. He was incredulous. So would anyone else have been. He wants to speak to the company and to the stewards, but I won't let him. As I told him, I have to continue to represent this constituency and work with these people when he and his team have departed.

It does make me worry, however, about the monthly meeting of the Knowsley Village branch of my party that I am due to speak at tomorrow evening. They've agreed to allow the meeting to be televised. Better still, they've said that they will be nominating me as their candidate, that they don't expect me to be opposed, and that they're happy for it to be filmed. This branch not only has the largest number of party members – more than 200 – it also has as many members as all but one of the other branches put together. It certainly has more members than the combined strength of the Militant-dominated branches, and it doesn't have any Militants of its own. What worries me now, though, is that the Militants might descend upon the meeting from other parts of the constituency and disrupt it. I'll warn them to expect trouble.

In the middle of all this I tried to concentrate on what I'd come to the Excelsior Hotel for. I had to prepare a line of questioning on the Government's record on law and order for a live Granada TV programme called *Under Fire* to be transmitted tonight. Willie Whitelaw was to be in the hot seat. He was to be interrogated by me, Peter Hennessy, a former journalist on *The Times* and now at the Policy Studies Institute, and Dennis Kavanagh, the Professor of Politics at Nottingham University.

I decided to concentrate on the number of riots we've experienced since the Tories came to power, on the massive 99 per cent increase in robbery, the 63 per cent increase in burglary, the 49 per cent increase in vandalism, the 40 per cent increase in serious crime and the 27 per cent increase in violence. I intended to tie this in with unemployment and his own statement, made in February 1978, that 'if boys and girls do not obtain jobs when they leave school they feel that society has no need for them. If they feel that,' he said, 'they do not see any reason why they should take part in that society and comply with its rules.' That was when unemployment was under the million. It's now just under four million.

I didn't expect him to answer the question, or even that I would catch him out. I knew him too well to expect that. He would just bluster his way through. All that I hoped was that by framing these statements as questions I might at least get over to the viewers the dismal Tory record on these issues.

Before the programme, Peter Hennessy and Dennis Kavanagh were more optimistic. At the meeting in the Granada TV Studios in Quay Street, Manchester, where we planned our attack, they exuded confidence. They really believed that they could corner him, trip him up, make him look stupid. Being academics, they expected him to be rational and to answer the questions. Some hope. They didn't listen to my warnings about how he would respond to some of their cherished but predictable questions.

It was a disaster. For us, that is, not for Willie. He enjoyed every moment and won every round. Mind you, he got off to a good start. He waddled into the studio where we and the audience were waiting and, a big smile on his face and his hand held out, said, 'Robert. How nice to see you.'

The programme went the same way. 'But you're a fair man,' he responded to one of my nastier jibes. 'You've always been prepared to give credit where it was due. You understand these matters . . .' He made me look a shit.

It was a polished and professional performance, just as I feared it would be. He exuded charm. He screwed us all, but especially me. Will I never learn?

Tuesday 8th October 1985

Peter Fisher is amazing. He has hidden depths. He's done a magnificent exercise on the delegates to the management committee.

When I arrived at his bungalow in Kirkby this morning he had long lists and diagrams spread across the dining room table with different coloured lines to indicate what stage of his vetting process each of the suspect delegates is at.

He had some good news. First, he's managed to identify all the T & G branches. There were some strange ones. Apparently 5/518 wasn't a typing error after all. The 5 represents the West Midland region. And it has to be a branch there, he said, because there's no 518 branch in the North West. He doesn't yet know where the branch is and if they know that they have sent a delegate to my constituency party. Inquiries, he smiled, are continuing.

'You realise, don't you?' he asked, 'that this has been organised?' I was sitting on his sofa while he paced the room. He was too agitated to sit down. 'Someone in the union has helped them. It's all been pushed through. You can see it,' he continued, 'by the composite branches. They're the branches that have been merged together to give them bigger membership and therefore more delegates. And they're from the unemployed centres. They're nearly all Militants. Smells, Robert, doesn't it?' He clapped his hands. He is enjoying the chase.

There is also the question of Phil McSorley. Phil is a long-standing member of the T & G, now retired. He used to be on the national executive of the union. He's been insisting to Peter and me for months that he is still a delegate to the constituency party and has complained of not receiving notices of meetings. I have always thought that, as he didn't appear on any recent list, he was mistaken. I assumed that he had probably been dropped by his branch, but they'd not actually told him. It could even have been a genuine administrative mistake.

'Oh no,' Peter said triumphantly. 'We can prove it. He's been a delegate all along. I've seen the copy of the letter in the correspondence book of the branch that nominated him as a delegate.' He was, he said, getting it copied before it got 'lost'.

I smiled.

'It's not funny,' he said. He was standing at the lace-curtained window looking into the narrow street. 'You've no idea what I'm uncovering. They're more than capable of ripping out the page if they find out that we know about it.'

Perhaps they are.

'Why do you think they've kept Phil McSorley off the GMC?' he asked. He faced me. 'Because they know that he'd support you, that's why. And there's another thing.' He was smiling again as he again paced the small living room. 'Interesting, isn't it, that of the 21 new delegates from the T & G, 13 of them live in the one ward?'

It was the ward where the secretary, the Beygas and the Militants lived and which they dominated. It's also the ward that Peter has represented as a councillor for the last eight years. Yet he doesn't recognise any of the names of the new delegates or know anything about them.

We agreed that we should challenge the credentials of all their . delegates. In particular, we are curious to know how the Militant supporter and constituency press officer, Dave Kerr, can be listed as a delegate from the Tobacco Workers' Union when he works for Liverpool City Council. It's also a little odd that so many former members of and delegates from the AUEW are now delegates from the notorious Militant-dominated and Liverpool-based Branch 5 of the GMBATU, the General and Municipal Workers Union. We shall have them all carefully looked at.

There was still more he had to tell. It concerned the chairman of the constituency, an open supporter of and newspaper seller for Militant. He has, apparently, been offering people membership of the T &G and a place on my management committee in return for a promise to support Tony Mulhearn. Fortunately, the chairman is not exactly what you would call bright. He approached one of my supporters. It seems he also deeply upset two delegates from Prescot by appearing without warning at the place where they work, asked to see them, and then canvassed for Mulhearn. They were angry, not just because of his tactics but also because they don't wish to be associated with the Militants, and certainly not at work.

I repeated much of this on film later in the day for Michael Cockerell when he interviewed me in a room in the Adelphi Hotel. I had to explain it all to him first, several times. I suppose it is both complicated and unusual for those not involved in the Labour party. They can't understand why a member of the Labour party would want to conspire against a Labour MP. It isn't part of their normal experience.

It was much easier for him this evening. He and his crew turned up as arranged at the meeting of the Knowsley Village branch of the party. The cameras, the lights and the crew seemed to dominate the

57

small wooden hall in Homer Road. I made a speech, answered questions and was nominated, without dissent, by the branch.

At the end of the meeting Michael Cockerell pulled a clever journalistic stunt. I had briefed him about the atmosphere of our constituency party meetings, and the way in which people are shouted down and intimidated and he wanted to speak to some of those at the receiving end of this treatment. I said that I would ask if they would talk to him but that it was unlikely that they would want to go on the record. They would be afraid of the repercussions. In fact, I thought that they ought not to go on film, even though it would be helpful to me if they did.

He bypassed all that. At the end of the meeting he went up to a group of women standing in the middle of the room and asked them what constituency meetings were like. They couldn't wait to tell him. They interrupted each other. Frances Bailey, Muriel Marsden, Doris Holmes and Edna Williams told the truth, and all the time the camera was filming.

I felt responsible for them, and I was concerned that they were not fully aware of what was happening. So I strode across the room, stood in front of the camera and stopped the proceedings. 'You realise,' I said, 'that this is all being recorded? Are you sure you want to do this?'

They insisted that they did. Bolstered by the membership of that group – and perhaps also by Neil's speech – they told the truth. It was good. It confirmed in the best possible way from the mouths of decent and credible witnesses all that I had been saying to Cockerell and others. Nevertheless, I felt guilty, and worried that they felt they had to do it for me.

Wednesday 9th – Thursday 10th October 1985

As if we haven't got enough problems! Now there's a black Labour council leader who seems to approve of what happened to the police during the riot at the Broadwater Farm Estate in Tottenham on Sunday evening.

During a police search of her home Mrs Cynthia Jarrett collapsed and died. In the ensuing riot the police were stoned and petrol-bombed. That has come to seem an almost normal reaction, but only recently. When I wrote about the police being petrol-bombed in

Liverpool in the manuscript of my 'masterpiece', *The Ceremony of Innocence: A Novel of 1984*, it was considered to be over-dramatic, but by the time it was published in 1983 Brixton and Toxteth had gone up in flames and what I had written seemed passé.

At Tottenham, however, there were two new and frightening developments. The police were shot at by youths with shotguns and one policeman, PC Blakelock, was hacked to death with knives. Nothing, but nothing, can justify any of that. Whatever the police may have done, however heavy-handed their search may have been, no matter what provocations they offered, there cannot be any excuse for the actions of the rioters. They must be caught, convicted and punished, and any self-respecting person should condemn them in the most uncompromising terms.

But what does Bernie Grant, the leader of Haringay Borough Council and prospective parliamentary Labour candidate for the safe seat of Tottenham, have to say? 'The police were to blame for what happened on Sunday night and what they got was a bloody good hiding.'

It's unbelievable. At first I thought that he was being misquoted or that it wasn't the Labour candidate but some Militant they'd brought in off the street with a petrol bomb still in one hand and a blood-stained knife in the other. But no, I was wrong. It was the leader of the Council speaking.

It's a disgrace. And Neil, thankfully, said so: he repudiated the remarks and disowned the man. But it's a nuisance that he is being put in that position more and more often, and has to be quick off the mark so that he can make ordinary decent people understand that the Bernie Grants do not speak for the real Labour party. The trouble is that some of what the Bernie Grants and the Liverpool Militants of this world do and say sticks to all of us. It will take a lot of living down. Only a firm voice from the top can provide any hope of an antidote.

Friday 11th October 1985

Great news. One of Peter Fisher's little 'investigations' has borne fruit. One of the Militants, Joe Lawler, a member of Hatton's private army (as the Liverpool static security service is known locally), a vice-chairman of the constituency party and the membership secretary, is not a delegate. It's fantastic news – he's one of the most uncouth, loudmouthed, nasty and active of them. But it's true. We double, treble, checked it. According to our source in the General & Municipal Workers Union, he hasn't been properly delegated all this time. To clinch it the union has sent a letter, dated 10th October, to the constituency secretary, Cathy Toner, appointing him as a delegate from yesterday. I bet she won't read that out at the next constituency meeting. This, of course, has always been our major problem. Because the constituency secretary works so closely with them we can't find out what's going on and it's easy for them to cover things up. She must, for example, have known he was not a delegate. She's been very active in challenging the credentials of all those who support me, even to the extent of having the impertinence to write to the EEPTU to ask how long its delegates have been members of the union. But I bet that she never wrote to the General and Municipal Workers Union about Lawler.

He's only one of five delegates listed as coming from the Militant-dominated GMBATU Liverpool 5 branch, all of whom are employed by Liverpool City Council. It's a coincidence, of course, that when there are 100,000 people unemployed on Merseyside three of the councillors on my management committee who support the Militants and Mulhearn have all recently got jobs with Liverpool City Council, just as it's a coincidence that three other members of the committee who express equally open and vigorous support for the Militants also work for the council – and that two of these have only recently been taken on. I wonder what it is about the members of my party that gives them that little bit extra, that makes them stand out from the other 100,000 Merseysiders competing for jobs, and enables them to succeed where so many others fail? It isn't that they have special skills. After all, you don't need that much experience or training to join the static security force or to be a grave digger or the like. We must ask them what it is. Others of my unemployed constituents should be let into the secret of success.

The elimination of Lawler doesn't make much difference to the arithmetic. It means there are now 141 delegates currently entitled to vote; I need a minimum of 71 votes, and I have 66. There's still a long way to go. We've got to wait for the results of the ASTMS inquiry and, most important of all, the sorting out of the T & G delegation.

Lawler's demise is more important than the removal of one vote, though – it's a morale boost. It shows how bad things are, the tricks they have got up to. It is amazing, after all, to find that the vice-chairman of the constituency party is not entitled to hold that office or even to attend meetings. Better still, he has participated in meetings that might now be considered invalid. Is the meeting that decided to go ahead with reselection valid if he attended? It seems doubtful. Is the annual general meeting valid? At the August management committee they won by one vote the motion to oppose the expulsion of Militants from the Labour party, so that's certainly invalid.

Interesting times are ahead.

The news that Heffer is not to stand for election to the Shadow Cabinet pales into insignificance in comparison, and so it should. Mind you, Heffer's not entirely stupid. He's seen the writing on the wall. It's not because he doesn't want to be a member of the Shadow Cabinet – of course he does; he'd like to be leader – but because he knows that he will not get elected. He only got 54 votes last year and he'd get even fewer now, after his Conference farce. Let's just hope that his little tantrum means that he's walked out of public life for good.

With all this, but especially Peter's news of Lawler and his hints of more to come racing through my mind, it was hard to concentrate during the long live lunchtime Granada TV magazine programme on prison reform. Sir Edward Gardner, the Tory MP for South Fylde, Andrew Rutherford, a lecturer in criminology at Southampton University, and I sat on a dais in front of a studio audience in Manchester and listened to convicted murderer Jimmy Boyle, and others, talking about the brutalising effects of prison.

They're right. The prison population has now reached an all-time record of nearly 48,000. The level of overcrowding is such that over a third of all prisoners are required to spend twenty-three of every twenty-four hours two or three to a cell built for one in Victorian times. They have no access to integral sanitary facilities and no opportunity to participate in work or education programmes. These conditions not only fail to meet the most elementary standards of human decency but they also violate internationally agreed standards for the treatment of prisoners. They make a mockery of the prison department's own stated aim of preparing prisoners to lead a good and useful life. There's not much chance of any rehabilitation work being done.

I said all this and more. It won't make me many friends, I don't suppose, but it needs saying.

Saturday 12th October 1985

We beat Southampton 1–0, as we should have done. The bad news is that Manchester United also won, beating QPR 2–0, so there's still a ten-point difference, but we'll close it.

Liverpool Militants, on the other hand, are on the way down and out. They've now decided not to issue redundancy notices to their workers but to lay them all off for four weeks before Christmas. How everyone is expected to manage without their wages and how this squares with the declared policy of protecting jobs and services is not explained.

Perhaps the bevy of national trade union leaders that are to visit the city and examine the books can knock their heads together and sort it all out. One of them is anonymously quoted as saying that there will be 'comradely discussions which could involve us placing our feet on the windpipes of some of the council leaders until they see sense.'

It looks promising, but it will take a long time, and even then I doubt if it will work. No-one outside Liverpool seems to have yet grasped the fact that the Militants do not want a solution. They're not looking for a settlement, because that would mean the drama was at an end. And it's the drama on which they thrive, both personally and politically.

Of course in one sense it doesn't really matter what happens now, they can't lose. If the Government capitulates and the money to cover Liverpool's deficit is found, then the Militants and their tactics will have been vindicated. Militancy pays. They will record another victory to set alongside that over Patrick Jenkin last year. Neil, the Labour party and all the rest of us will stand condemned as cautious wimps, fainthearts and cowards. People of the past. And if the money to balance Liverpool's budget isn't found they will see it as the fault not just of the Tories but of the trade union leaders and Neil Kinnock for not fully supporting them. It's Scargill all over again. It's their victory if they succeed, and everyone else's fault if they fail.

Apart from all this, the Militants have actually achieved their main objective, which was to politicise, radicalise and mobilise more people in 'the struggle', as they call it. They now have a strong base of mass support, especially amongst the young and the unemployed. The portents for the future are ominous – not just for the Labour party, but for all of us.

The Tories have a lot to answer for. Their spiteful and callous economic policies have caused places like Liverpool to be written off and have created a permanent pool of unemployed and increasingly unemployable people. In my own borough of Knowsley, for instance, only six per cent of last year's school leavers actually went into full-time employment. 68 per cent of all school children in the borough are in receipt of free school meals, 61 per cent of the school population is in receipt of some help with school clothing, 80 per cent of council tenants, in virtually a 90 per cent council house borough, receive some help with their rent, and more than 50 per cent of all households are in receipt of state benefits. Over half of the 18-and 19-year olds have never had a full-time job.

You can't consign young people to the dole queue immediately they leave school, let them marry and have children on the dole, hold out no prospect of their ever being a positive and contributing part of society, of ever living any hint of the life portrayed daily in full-colour advertisements on their television screens, and then express surprise when they're attracted to the glib and easy slogans, the drama, the excitement and, above all, the action offered by the Militants. What is really surprising, as I've said several times in the last few years when debating unemployment in the House, is that it hasn't happened before. They've nothing to lose. They don't own their homes, they have no job, no prospect of a job – ever – and no money. What have they to be grateful for? What do they owe society? As Willie Whitelaw said when in opposition in 1978, you can't shut young people out of normal society and then expect them to obey its rules.

Whatever the outcome to the sad farce in Liverpool we have to deal with the economic and social problems now or suffer the horrendous consequences for our failure. It's getting late.

Sunday 13th October 1985

We had hoped that our friends Ruth Jackson and Guy East would be able to go with us to see *Subway*, but they were busy. We went alone to the Chelsea Cinema, after dropping Natasha in Baker Street. She was off to see the *Rocky Horror Show* and would be staying in town. She has a good and varied social life. Dominic, on the other hand, is more like me – home-loving.

But back to *Subway*. It's a stylish and entertaining film, one that both Natasha and Dominic would enjoy. Indeed, the audience was extremely young. We feel older all the time. It wasn't as good as *Desperately Seeking Susan*, which we saw earlier this week with Ruth and Guy at the Kensington Odeon, and after which we had supper in Geale's Fish Restaurant in Farmer Street in Notting Hill. Nor did it have the depth or menace of *La Balance*, with which I couldn't help but compare it. But it was relaxing, if only for a time. Even during some of the most visually exciting parts of the film, like the car chase, I found myself thinking about Peter Fisher's discoveries of what has been happening in the T & G to get delegates who are opposed to me on to my general committee. It's still slightly unbelievable. No-one I've spoken to about it, including Tony Bevins really believes it: I don't believe it myself sometimes.

Jan does. We talked about it as we walked the dog in the woods this afternoon. Jan, as always, was collecting material for her dried flower arrangements, as always, while the dog lagged sadly behind. She's riddled with cancer. Jan seems to spend a great deal of time with her at the vet's. He says that we shall have to have her put down soon, but we're resisting. She's part of the family. The house wouldn't have the same tone or character without her. While we're sure she's in no pain we'll continue to pay the bills and suffer the unsightly nature of her 'sores'.

The film that Michael Cockerell is making is also worrying me. It's difficult to see how they will portray me because I haven't yet got a feel of the angle they've adopted or the kind of story that they've decided to tell. Jan keeps telling me not to worry. 'Just tell the truth,' has become her refrain. But I do worry, because I've enough knowledge of journalists and television to know how they can twist and distort the truth without actually lying. The nastier experiences that some of my colleagues have been subjected to have shown me how unscrupulous the media can be in using you just for the sake of the story.

I decide I must be more positive, more assertive, more confident. Or is it 'bloody, bold and resolute'?

Monday 14th October 1985

We're in trouble.

According to my well-placed and well-informed source in the T & G, active efforts are being made within the union to deliver my seat to the Militants. Well, well, well. My expectation that the T & G regional bureaucracy would be aghast at what is happening in my constituency and act swiftly to sort it out has been destroyed. Now I understand how the Militants have got away with it: they've had no anxiety about being uncovered. No wonder they have been so blatant.

It means, to begin with, that we can expect no help from the union. If we're to uncover any breaches of union rules or nomination procedures we'll have to do it ourselves and in the face of officials who will be quick to hide the infractions of the rules. It's going to be difficult, if not impossible, to prove anything now.

But there's worse. I've found out that the man Peter Killeen is liaising with in the T & G to investigate the credentials of the T & G's delegates is actually the man responsible for organising it all. Christ.

Apparently Peter Killeen approached the official saying that the T & G had more delegates to my constituency party than it was entitled to and more than it had paid affiliation fees for. Peter Killeen asked him to sort it out, and to reduce the delegation. The official then apparently went back to the union, instructed that all communications between the Labour party and the union over Knowsley North must be referred to him and, most importantly, tried to find ways in which the union could increase its subscription so as to keep all its delegates in place even at this late hour.

This was so important that I had to speak to Killeen. I phoned him at the headquarters of the Labour Party in Salford.

'Oh no,' he exclaimed. I could tell he was shocked. 'Are you sure?'

I gave him the name of the union official and enough details of what was happening to convince him.

'I don't believe it,' he exclaimed.

'Neither did I,' I said. 'But what other explanation can there be? You see him, you tell him they've got too many delegates and will he reduce their number and he goes away and tries to find ways of making them legitimate instead.'

'But he can't do it. It's not possible now,' Peter said, as if to himself.

'I know,' I responded. 'But the fact that he's trying shows he's not playing by the rules, that he's not on my side, doesn't it?'

'Yes.' He said it quietly. I could almost feel the sense of shock, hear his brain functioning.

'My informant has always been right before and has no reason to mislead me, so I have to trust him. At least,' I concluded, 'be careful how much you let them know.'

He promised to do that. He's probably another one who now thinks I'm paranoid.

Tuesday 15th to Thursday 17th October 1985

I wrote to Neil to say that I was resigning as Shadow Home Office Minister. I have no regrets. I've thought about it for some time. Indeed, apart from my reselection problem I seem to have thought about little else for the last few days. Jan thinks that I'm making a big mistake but she accepts that I'm determined.

I wrote to Neil instead of asking to see him because, as I said in my letter, I didn't want to waste his time. I also didn't want to give him an opportunity of dissuading me, this time. It means that I will be off the front bench and out of serious politics at a senior level for the rest of this Parliament. It also means that I will not be a minister when the next Labour Government is formed, as I could reasonably have expected to be. It is a serious political setback, at the very least, but I felt happier once I had written and posted the letter.

There are several reasons why I feel that I have to resign. The most important is the battle for reselection, which is taking a lot of my time. I never seem to be off the telephone. It is also distracting and debilitating. No-one who hasn't been through it can fully appreciate

66

just how horrible and distasteful the whole thing is, and how it saps your confidence and motivation.

I'm not the only one. Frank Field, the MP for Birkenhead, who fought off a sustained challenge from Militant, says that it took two years out of his life. He feels very bitter and angry about the whole thing and the way in which he was made to suffer. He has a right to feel like that: it was an unnecessary and disgraceful waste of his time and talent that could have been more usefully employed in Parliament on behalf of his constituents and the party. Another MP, this time from the so-called hard left in the North, actually shed tears, real, wet, tears, on the shoulders of a colleague in the Tea Room in the House of Commons, because of the strain of being opposed, even though he knew he would win. Norman Atkinson, the MP for Tottenham for the last couple of decades and former Treasurer of the Labour party, who was deselected in favour of Bernie Grant, of all people, says that the reselection process took him out of politics for a year.

Reselection is, indeed, the dominant and often the sole topic of conversation amongst my colleagues in the Tea Room, at dinner and in the bars, at the House of Commons. No-one seems capable of talking about anything else. And these are colleagues who are unopposed, who will be reselected from a short-list of one as I was in my Ormskirk constituency. Nevertheless they feel that a threat exists: something could happen, things could go wrong. There is always the possibility that they will do or say something – or be forced by events, like the miners' strike, into a public position – that will put them temporarily at odds with their constituency party and so lose them the nomination. There is a great incentive, as they say, 'to keep their heads down'.

They have sleepless nights. They are constantly looking over their shoulders, spend more time in their constituencies on party politics and have to devote more time and energy to organising their supporters when they should be in Parliament. As they have all reiterated dozens of times, we will not be able to run a Labour Government in these circumstances, especially if more of my colleagues are confronted with the kind of conflict I have now.

Imagine, for example, the position that Gerald Kaufman would have been in had he been Home Secretary, or Peter Shore as Leader of the House. Or, better still, Mike Cocks as Chief Whip trying to organise the vote in the House – with perhaps a minority Labour

Government – and his own bloody reselection battle raging all around him. It would be impossible. You can't give proper attention to important political issues at Westminster or in Whitehall when full-time politicians in the constituency are working out of fully-equipped offices – called an Unemployed Centre – to besmirch your reputation and blacken your character.

It will be worse still if every action of the Labour Government requiring the support and the votes of its MPs is subject to the approval of constituency parties who have the ultimate sanction of deselection to impose on those MPs who do not back the constituency line and vote against the Government. The only way to prevent all this is to introduce, before the next Labour government, one-man-one-vote for all party members in the constituency when reselection takes place.

But back to the present. As a consequence of my reselection problems, I've not given the time to my Front Bench duties that I should have done. I haven't carried out my responsibilities in the way that I am capable of and which the leader and the Party have a right to expect, and I told Neil so. I'm conscious all the time that I'm not doing justice to the job, to the Home Office team, or to the Party.

Jan and Tony Bevins insist that no-one else thinks that. I hope they're right, but it doesn't matter. I know that I've been falling down on the job, at least by my own standards. I know that I could have done better, and that's enough.

But I have to admit that the joy has gone. That's the real tragedy. Politics has been spoilt, I hope only temporarily. It is difficult, after all, to be excited about policy initiation and political battles when, all the time, there's a little group within your own constituency party that is gnawing away at your foundations, trying to catch you out, find you at fault, undermine you. It sours everything. The real battle is to ensure that it doesn't sour me, that I don't become an embittered, cynical and sad old man.

It's strange how things go full circle. I can vividly remember the way I felt in 1983 when I hadn't got a shadow ministerial job. It was November, after the Conference, the recess, and the first Shadow Cabinet election of Neil's leadership. I'd expected a job, but I didn't get one. Throughout that day, as the junior appointments were becoming known, virtually every person I saw wanted to know what job I'd got. 'What have you been offered?', 'What have you got?' seemed to be the opening lines of every conversation. Indeed, that sombre November day the question became not so much 'Which job have you got?', but 'How many offers have you had?' I alone, or so it seemed, not only did not have a job but had not even had an offer – even one that could be withdrawn or refused.

That hurt. It would be foolish and a lie to pretend that it did not. I felt irrelevant and unwanted. It was like failing the 11+ examination all over again. It was difficult, indeed impossible, to be part of the little groups and conclaves that formed in the dark corners of the long Commons corridors to discuss the latest appointments when you were no part of the process.

Any hopes that I might have entertained of being a part of the Home Office team were quashed when it became known that Denis Howell, the former Minister of Sport and MP for Birmingham Small Heath, and Alf Dubs, the MP for Battersea, had been appointed. 'Why did you turn it down?' several incredulous colleagues and journalists asked me. I think they thought I was being ridiculously honourable in saying that it hadn't been offered to me.

Giles Radice, the shadow Secretary of State for Education and MP for North Durham, made a particular effort to seek me out and to commiserate with me for not having been included in Neil's new team. He was the only person to do so. He is a good man, but I did think that I had other friends. Perhaps they found it too embarrassing.

Giles was concerned to ensure that I did not respond to not being given a job by opting out – that was certainly a strong initial temptation. He also had several reasons to offer as to why I had not been taken on board. I don't know now whether he had heard them from others or had made his own assessment. Anyway, they were (a) that I had voted for Michael Meacher, the MP for Oldham West, instead of Roy Hattersley, the MP for Birmingham, Sparkbrook, in the deputy leadership contest; (b) that I was too flippant and had hurt 'important' people by some of the things that I had said to and about them; (c) that I did not belong to an identifiable group in the parliamentary party and did not have a powerful 'patron' to bat for me; and (d) that I was too 'grand'. I did not understand what he meant by being 'grand'. Giles said that I gave the impression of knowing it all, that I was too self-assured when speaking or asking questions in the chamber and that I did not make mistakes. Well, that's true, I suppose.

The consolation that day was Frank Longford breezing into the meeting of Parliamentary Penal Affairs Group that I was chairing in the Jubilee Room near Westminster Hall saying loudly: 'Robert, I'm really enjoying your book. It's very good, very interesting. But why is it so short? I want it to go on longer! Have you read it?' he asked the assembled and bemused company of the Lords Avebury, Donaldson, Hunt, Ullswater and Kagan and the Baronesses Birk and David, amongst others, as well as several MPs like Douglas Hogg and Jeremy Hanley. I don't think that any of them bought a copy of my novel as a result.

Mind you, that period did have its lighter moments. While still in bed one Sunday morning I got a call from Barry Jones, the MP for Alyn and Deeside. Would I vote for him in the Shadow Cabinet elections, he asked? I was taken aback. We didn't know each other that well.

'It's my first time,' he explained, 'and I don't want to be humiliated.' I said that I would vote for him if he would vote for me. He said he had one vote spare and that I could have it.

A couple of days later Jeff Rooker and I compared notes on who we had voted for. We sat alongside each other in the deep green armchairs in the Tea Room whispering out of the corners of our mouths like Militants. We had both voted for Denis Healey, Peter Shore, Gerald Kaufman, John Smith, Giles Radice, Jack Cunningham, John Golding and John Silkin, amongst others, and each other, of course. Barry Jones was one of my 'others'. I told Jeff about the phone call.

Jeff laughed. 'Hang on a minute,' he said, hardly able to contain himself. 'What time did you say he rang you?'

'Sunday morning,' I said, puzzled.

'You sure?' He was now laughing aloud.

'Yes.'

'Well, there's something funny going on here. He rang me too. Only he rang me on Sunday evening and said he had two votes spare.'

We laughed at his cheek. Both of us had voted for him. What we didn't know when we were laughing was that he was to be elected. It surprised everyone. We knew then, too late, how it's done.

I remember, too, when I was appointed to the Front Bench in January 1984, as Home Affairs spokesman. I was pleased. So it seems was everyone else. When I stood at the despatch box for the first time at Home Office Question Time there were loud – I thought perhaps slightly ironic – cheers from our side and the Tories joined in. It was several seconds before I was able to make myself heard. Douglas Hurd, as I see now from Hansard, recorded the fact by saying: 'The House is clearly delighted at the election of the honourable Member for Knowsley North to the Opposition Front Bench.'

Dennis Skinner also got into the act. 'You've only got five years left, Robert,' he called out loudly. As always his timing was impeccable. Everyone was convulsed with laughter just as I was about to speak.

They were exciting times, but not any more. I have to be honest: being on the Front Bench, certainly in my position, has not exactly been exhilarating. The job hasn't been up to much. I haven't had responsibility for those things I actually know about and have established a reputation for, like prisons, criminal justice policy, the police and civil liberty issues. Instead, I've had the riveting subjects of civil defence, censorship, animal experiments, data protection, broadcasting and drugs. All important subjects, I don't deny that – but not particularly scintillating ones, and certainly not at the forefront of political debate and controversy.

The result has been that I get called once at each Home Office Question Time if the Tories – and particularly the obsessive Neil Thorne, Tory MP for Ilford South, who seems to be dedicated to improving our system of civil defence – have bothered to put down a question on the subject. When I was on the backbenches the speaker would call me twice or sometimes three times, and on issues of my choice. Worse is that I cannot speak in the debates on the major bills that, as a backbencher, I would automatically have contributed to. The irony is that I shall probably now be more active as a backbencher than I have been as a front bencher.

Neil is in Austria. Dick Clements, his assistant and former editor of *Tribune*, rang to say that Neil has received my letter. He asked me not to do anything or say anything to anyone. Although I said it wasn't necessary Dick insisted that Neil wants to speak to me. I will see him on Monday if he doesn't call me over the weekend.

Meanwhile the *Liverpool Echo* and the Liverpool *Daily Post* both carried big stories about the reselection saga after I spoke at their request to the *Echo's* Andy Grice and the *Post's* David Utting. The former has a two-page spread about me, Frank Field and Sean Hughes, my neighbour in Knowsley South, under the banner headline 'Militant: The Path to Parliament'. The 'Front Bench Home

Affairs spokesman', it says of me, is keeping his tactics close to his chest but 'reveals' that he would 'consider' standing as an 'independent' against a Militant candidate were one to be selected.

No, I wouldn't. Not as an independent'. I'm Labour. When I stand for parliament again I will stand as a Labour candidate and no other. This was the first time that I'd hinted at standing against a Militant, although I had been thinking about it for some time. I have also been pressured by many in my local party to make such a decision. Pressed by Andy Grice as to what I would do if Mulhearn was selected, I said that I would 'consider' standing against him.

In the Liverpool *Daily Post* the next morning David Utting turned this into me 'hurling down a gauntlet to Militant Tendency supporters seeking to oust' me. In fact, of course, it's the inescapable and logical outcome of what is happening. As I said to David Utting, if membership of the Militant Tendency is incompatible with membership of the Labour party, as the Labour Party and Conference say that it is, then I would be failing in my duty if I were to allow such a candidate ever to masquerade as a Labour candidate, let alone become a Labour MP.

I admit, I do feel strongly that I ought not to allow my constituents to be manipulated, exploited and taken over by the revolutionaries of the Trotskyite Militant Tendency. I also feel that I have the right to expect support from the Labour party at all levels for that point of view. But will I get it?

Friday 18th and Saturday 19th October 1985

So now I know what the charges against me are. All the organising, all the conspiring, all the fixing, all the manoeuvering, all the shouting and the intimidation, all the trickery, all the hate is because I don't live in the constituency. That's what Michael Cockerell said, anyway. That was the complaint the Militants put to him when he interviewed them in the Kirkby Unemployed Centre in Leeside Avenue, Kirkby, and which he now put to me from behind the TV camera as we stood in a cold wind outside a derelict factory on the Knowsley Industrial Estate.

As I said then, they really must be scraping the bottom of the barrel if that's the best that they can do. No, I don't live in the constituency, nor have I for the last dozen years, though we did have a flat in Ormskirk. I've made no secret of the fact. Indeed, I told my party when I was first selected that if I were elected I would move house and live near the place I was expected to work five days a week, and that is what I did. Unlike many of my colleagues on Merseyside who appear to live in their constituencies, I was unashamed about the fact that I expected to live where I had to work and to have my family there with me. My family comes first – before politics – and I did not intend to become an absentee father. I even announced our move to the press. It was on the front pages of the local newspapers in 1974.

All right, so some members of the party complained. I met their moans head-on at the next management committee. I was unrepentant about the decision – as I am still – but said that I would always be in the constituency and at meetings when I was needed. 'If ever I'm absent without good reason from the constituency when I'm supposed to be here,' I said, 'then you can complain.'

And they never have, neither in the party, at meetings or on the doorsteps. I've been re-elected every time since February 1974, and for good reason. Though I say it myself, I've been a good constituency MP, perhaps partly because I know of my vulnerability to criticism for living outside the constituency.

I said much of this in response to Michael Cockerell's questions, conscious though I was that it would be too long and complicated for inclusion in his film. Television, unfortunately, deals in images and seconds. In this particular format, it's not capable of encompassing a reasoned explanation. When he first put the question, I replied, 'Neither, so far as I know, does Eric Heffer, Allan Roberts, Bob Wareing or Tony Benn, but I don't hear these complaints directed at them.' That, I suspect, is the bit they will actually use – it's more pungent and to the point than a long, rambling, personal explanation.

There was also a secondary complaint against me, which was that I hadn't done enough about unemployment. I haven't brought work to the area. Now how do you answer that?

Well, let's try. MPs don't actually have the power to bring jobs to a place. I think the Militants actually know that. I'm sure that they are not so stupid as not to know; indeed, they're clever enough to pretend it's simple so as to be able to say that I've failed. But if I have failed then so has every other Liverpool MP, including their beloved Terry Fields in neighbouring Broadgreen. The level of unemploy-

73

ment in their constituencies is similar and in some cases worse than in mine.

In fact, the Militants and their ilk in Liverpool are the biggest deterrents to job creation on Merseyside that there have ever been. Dozens of times in the last few years I have tried fruitlessly to persuade companies that I knew were looking for sites for new plants to locate on Merseyside and in Knowsley. On a couple of occasions I've actually escorted the decision-makers around the area, pointed out its industrial estates, the good communications by road and air, its pleasant places to live, and, despite appearances to the contrary, its good record of industrial relations. They were impressed, particularly so on one occasion. We were put on the shortlists on which we never usually figure. But each time the decision went against us, because of their perception of our militancy. It didn't matter that we aren't as militant or as strike-prone as they thought: they made their decision, in this instance at least, on the basis of their beliefs rather than on the facts.

I didn't say all that. How could I? It would have taken far too long. I merely asked people to look at my record, which is not bad in drawing attention to the terrible problem of unemployment that we have. After all, I escorted 25 of my unemployed young constituents to see the Prime Minister in Downing Street recently. I've fought against every closure and redundancy, and there have been lots of both; and at least until I was appointed to the Front Bench, I think, I spoke in every single debate on unemployment in the House of Commons since I was elected.

But it's so easy to destroy all that. If one person appears on television and says 'he doesn't do anything about unemployment', that is what the watching millions will believe. I will not be given time to tell them how we saved the jobs at the Kirkby co-operative for four years, or how hundreds of jobs at Otis Elevator were preserved, and all the rest.

In many ways, though, it was a relief. Is that all? I asked myself as I climbed into my car and drove away from the television team. Is that really the best they can do? I couldn't wait to tell Jan – and Peter. They wouldn't believe it either. I can live with those two complaints, criticisms, call them what you will, because I know them both to be unfounded and silly.

I visited an old lady living on the tenth floor of a block of flats who wanted to see me but could not get to my surgeries. She was housebound and lonely. She reminded me of my maternal grand-mother, who had had to wait until she was a widow of 80 before being moved from her Victorian slum in Lennox Street, Lozells, Birmingham, to a new pensioner's flat in Hockley. She was inordinately proud of it. For the first time in her life she not only had a kitchen, a bathroom and a lavatory, she also had central heating. But she was lonely and isolated on the sixth floor, afraid to open the front door and, just like my constituent, shut off from the warmth and gossip of her neighbours.

My constituent wanted a transfer back to Liverpool so she could be near her relatives. Many of my constituents come from Liverpool and a lot of them want to go back, although few succeed. They're only a mile or so from Liverpool's boundary, in this case a few hundred yards, but they might as well be in a foreign country. The bureaucracy says that they can't transfer. It will be difficult to get this woman the simple move that she needs. The system is absurd.

I was thinking the whole time about the interview with Michael Cockerell. Why, I wondered, didn't the Militants tell the truth? Why didn't they say they didn't like my politics? That's the real issue: it's ideological. They're Militants and I'm not. They're believers in the politics of the street and of the mob, whereas I believe in old-fashioned things like the rule of law and parliamentary democracy. Strange, isn't it, how they of all people won't actually stand up for what they believe in? Are they really that ashamed? No doubt they are. That's why they've infiltrated the Labour party – the public won't have them for themselves.

They certainly can't confess the other reason that they want to be rid of me, which is that they have no control over me. I don't support their motions and resolutions, I won't buy the Militant newspaper, I won't subscribe to their notions of how an MP should behave, I don't give money to the constituency party or ten per cent of my income to them as Terry Fields and Dave Nellist, the Militant-supporter MPs do. I won't endorse irresponsible foolishness like the strike of schoolchildren that they organised in Kirkby, which led to young boys being put into police cells and charged with breaches of the peace while the Militants went scot-free. I won't say that convicted jailed miners should be released, that secret ballots are a bad thing, and that violence, especially on picket lines, is justified and acceptable. I certainly will not condemn the civil and common law as 'Tory law' or the courts as 'capitalist courts'. They're my laws and my courts and I will defend them both.

It's my point-blank refusal to do all these things when my colleagues in neighbouring constituencies acquiesce that rankles with them. Naturally, I must be a great irritant, just like Frank Field and my friend in St Helens, John Evans. If I was a Militant I would want to get rid of us all – and Sean Hughes as well. Surviving is easy. Anyone can survive. All that's necessary is to do as you are told.

Mine isn't the only constituency on Merseyside that has been overrun by Militant. Most have, especially in Liverpool, so the Militants could get rid of Heffer and Wareing and Loyden and Parry tomorrow if they wanted to. They could probably dump Allan Roberts as well if they tried. But why should they, when they receive political support from all these MPs most of the time?

The dockers seem to be untainted, at any rate: the docks branch of the T & G has nominated me. No doubt Peter Fisher, who gave me the news of his branch, had a lot to do with it, since it's the branch from which he's a delegate. But it is interesting. That's the working class, the actual manual workers. They have no problem about saying, as Peter reported, 'that Kilroy-Silk does a good job', and in unanimously nominating me.

Nor are they the only ones. Another branch of the party in Kirkby has nominated me; so have several branches of the EEPTU, UCATT, the Fabian Society, the Women's Council, the Co-operative Party, and the Society of Labour Lawyers. More will follow.

The branches representing the so-called unemployed, based on the unemployed centres, are the ones that seem to have difficulties. I wonder why? It couldn't be, I suppose, that they're the ones that the Militants dominate? Other than that, as Peter said when we lunched on Friday in his home, 'It's gone quiet.' We're still waiting for the results of our requests to our various sources for more information.

It looks as if Chloe will have to be put down. We tried to take her for a walk on Saturday, but we didn't get far; she straggled behind us with what seemed to be great difficulty. The deterioration in her condition has been sudden and dramatic. We turned back, put her in the house, and went ahead with our walk without her. It wasn't the same.

We got back home just in time for the football results. I switched on the television to hear that we had drawn away at Manchester United. Chelsea lost, fortunately, so we're still second.

Sunday 20th October 1985

The continuing good weather seduced us into the garden again, although there is very little work to be done other than the seemingly never-ending job of leaf collecting. I think they all find their way here from nearby Burnham Beeches. Actually there's a great deal that needs doing but in the interests of the bird life we deliberately leave it until the spring. Thus the Golden Rod, the Michaelmas Daisies, the Rudbekia, the Cosmos and all the rest that should be either cut down or uprooted are left to provided the birds with winter food. They're also helped by the corn scattered on the lawn for my doves: a surprise fortieth birthday gift, together with the dovecote, from Jan.

Our reward is a garden filled in winter and early spring with a succession of various finches and tits, and the special delight of regular visits from pairs of firecrests and goldcrests. The disadvantage, which we cheerfully suffer, is that there is so much more work in the spring when we're clearing up and planting out almost simultaneously.

My mother rang from her home in Birmingham, as she always does on Sundays. She was worried about my sister Madeline who lives in Porthcawl. There wasn't anything particular to worry about, it was just that she hadn't heard from her for a couple of days and Madeline wasn't answering her phone.

It's sad how quickly circumstances change and close families disintegrate. It's less than a year ago that we were all in my sister's new house, built by her husband, David. It was very impressive. They had only been in residence a week. There was a lot of work still to be done, and before long we were all at it. I painted the French windows, using the skill I acquired when I and Barry Sheerman, now the MP for Huddersfield, started and ran a decorating business in Sunbury-on-Thames during one vacation from LSE. Jan grouted the kitchen tiles, Natasha scraped paint and plaster off the sinks and lavatories, Mum and her third husband, Ray, scraped and cleaned windows, David filled in holes in the garden paths, my two young nephews, Duncan and Jon-Daniel cleared the garden of rubbish, and Madeline cooked the meals and made tea. We all worked for a whole weekend.

It was a good family get-together, but there will be no more like it. My sister is divorced and Ray died in April. Within months the character of our close family has changed fundamentally. It means that Madeline visits us less often and I don't get to see the boys. I miss them.

There's also a blight on Christmas. We used to play host to the whole family: Jan's mother, her husband, Colin, my mother and Ray, my sister and her husband and the two boys and, often my own father's younger sister and her husband and daughter, and my stepfather's younger brother and wife. They all get on well together; they've known each other a long time. This year it looks as if we shall have only our mothers and Colin.

Monday 21st October 1985

Started running – sorry, jogging – again today. It was hard work. I don't know why but I only run when Parliament is in session. We started back today after the summer recess and the party conferences, so I haven't run my thrice weekly one-and-three-quarter miles in less than the twelve minutes ordained by the health freaks since July. It took me fourteen minutes this morning.

It's not the physical exercise that I go for, though I have to admit that I always feel better, more relaxed, when I have been jogging. What really attracts me is the quiet country lanes in which, no matter how many times I travel along them, there is always something different to see. So it was today.

It was a beautiful, balmy morning: a thin sun and a warm wind. There was a heavy scent of pine needles. And something I've never seen before: a flock of pied wagtails. I've seen them singly and in pairs but never in flocks. I counted well over a dozen.

Later, work began again in the House. Following a complaint from a constituent at one of my surgeries during the recess about the quality of drinking water, and her assertion that it was polluted in the North West, I tabled a series of parliamentary questions to the Secretary of State for the Environment. Angela Rumbold, the junior Environment Minister and MP for Mitcham and Morden, answered them today, and the replies make interesting reading. My constituent was right. According to the Minister the North West Water Authority has one or more water supply areas which exceeds

78

the limit laid down by the European Economic Community directive on drinking water in respect of aluminium, manganese, iron and lead. It will not, the Minister said, be in a position to comply with the European standards until 1990.

I shall have to pursue this matter to ensure that the date is not allowed to slip. There is no reason why my constituents should have to drink water inferior to that produced in other parts of the country. Nor, indeed, do I see why we should be prepared to accept standards lower than those in operation in other parts of Europe. This seems to be a neglected, though interesting, subject. In researching it after meeting my constituent I was surprised to learn of the existence of so many private water supplies. The answers to my parliamentary questions reveal that there are known to be 80,000 such supplies in the United Kingdom, mostly in rural areas serving single properties. About 200 private supplies regularly service more than 500 people. These, apparently, give the most cause of concern, especially as potential sources of disease. I shall table further questions. Noni, my researcher, insists that she also should pursue the matter, as she finds it both interesting and disturbing.

Everyone seems pleased to be back at the Commons. It's like returning to school after the summer holidays. Even the Tories nod and enquire if we've had a 'good recess'. I said yes, but it wasn't true.

Tuesday 22nd October 1985

This month's routine meeting of my constituency management committee in the Unemployed Centre in the redundant school in Kirkby tonight was as nasty and as ill-tempered as most of the others have been for the last two years. Not that I was surprised, especially as it was the Militant's first opportunity to display their anger at Neil's demolition of the Liverpool Militants at Conference.

Someone, I'm not sure whether it was Peter Fisher or Geoff Kneale, had suggested that this would be a better, more sensible meeting. They would, he had prophesied 'behave themselves' because of the sudden increase in press interest in our affairs and the presence of Michael Cockerell and his film team in the area.

But they didn't behave themselves – they acted as usual. That is to say that in addition to the habitual shouting, the heckling and the barracking of opponents, and the general uproar, the Militant-led majority criticised the Labour party at every opportunity, attacked Neil on every pretext, and abused me as a matter of course.

There was a time – throughout the decade of the existence of the Ormskirk constituency – when I enjoyed attending the monthly meetings in the then Kirkby Labour Club in St Chad's Drive, Kirkby. I actually looked forward to them: they were opportunities to meet those party members I might not have seen for a couple of weeks, to catch up on the gossip and to have a friendly and relaxed drink afterwards with people who were comrades and friends. But there was more than that, too. The whole atmosphere within the party and at meetings was different then. It was welcoming, open, friendly and co-operative. The debates and, yes, the fierce arguments were conducted in a civilised and a comradely manner. We were all in the same party working towards the same objectives: we were aware of it and we behaved accordingly.

That is no longer the case in Knowsley North, where there are now two parties. There is the Labour party and there's the rabble that belongs to the ranters and the Militants. Indeed, after tonight's meeting a large group of members of the 'real' Labour party insisted upon seeing me. They had had enough. 'We're not going on with this,' they said, as we stood outside the Unemployment Centre in the cold and dark. I could feel the damp infiltrating the soles of my shoes. 'This isn't the Labour party. There's no place for us here,' they said. They huddled inside their overcoats.

What they want – and what they still half-intend, despite all my protestations when we continued the discussion later at the home of one of them in Prescot – is to have their own separate meetings. They are tired, they said, of being disregarded and treated with contempt when they actually represent a majority of the members of the party and the overwhelming number of Labour voters. They are 'sick', to use their word, of not being allowed to speak and of being jeered at, villified and verbally abused when they do speak. They're afraid of the atmosphere of menace and intimidation and of the occasional threats of violence, such as happened again tonight. They want no more of meetings that invariably degenerate into uproar and always border on chaos. They are disheartened by the way in which decisions on resolutions and other matters are decided by votes, whose accuracy they dispute, and of how people seem to vote several times and go in and out of separate doors casting votes as they come and go; at the way in which their resolutions and their nominees for

80

office are constantly and ruthlessly rejected; at the way in which meetings are allowed to drag on well after their allocated time; of the way in which 'emergency' resolutions then appear for the first time, in clear breach of the rules, and get voted through. And challenging the breach of the rules cuts no ice: the Militants simply vote that it is not a breach. My supporters also complain at the way in which the meetings are deliberately engineered so that there is no time for me to make my parliamentary report and that when I insisted upon making one I have to speak briefly, conscious that if I do not then my supporters will miss their lifts home.

They are angry and upset. 'There's no point in coming here,' they said. 'We'll have our own meetings.'

'You can't,' I insisted, desperately. 'That's called leaving the Labour party.'

'No, it's not,' they retorted. They were indignant. 'We're the Labour party. That lot aren't the Labour party,' they almost shouted as one. 'They have nothing at all to do with socialism. They're not *our* Labour party.'

They were right, of course, but they would be playing into the hands of the Militants if they did have separate meetings. I think I've persuaded them not to, for the moment. At least they've promised not to do anything without speaking to me again. It's alarming. I not only understand the way they feel, I agree with them. In many ways it would be the sensible and logical thing to do, but they mustn't do it. As I said, they've got to stay and fight.

The troops are demoralised, and so would anyone else be. There's no comradeship, no co-operation, no tolerance, no democracy, still less any real debate in the constituency party. The real Labour party, for example, would never deliberately deny two of its ten branches that have between them over fifty per cent of the constituency party's members from having any representation on the District Labour party. But this lot have done just that. They even giggled when they did it, as if it were some great joke.

There is some doubt as to whether their action is constitutional. There's no doubt that it's blatantly unfair. It would never have happened before, not just because there was no Militant-dominated caucus with totalitarian propensities who'd want to do it, but because there existed a real sense of fair play, a notion of give and take, of compromise and tolerance. Indeed, that feeling existed to such an extent that the only two Militants then in the area, one of

81

whom is the constituency chairman now, were allowed to occupy a disproportionate amount of the constituency's time. They were always given the floor to air their views and treated with respect and consideration.

There's a lesson here. It's a hard one to learn, but I've learnt it. Never, the lesson says, tolerate for a moment in a democracy those that seek to subvert or destroy it. If you do, and they prosper and grow, they will ruthlessly attempt to eliminate all opposition to them, as they have done here. 'Tolerance', as Woodrow Wilson reminded us, 'is an admirable intellectual gift; but it is of little worth in politics.' But then I actually believed in what he scathingly refers to as a 'meaningless courtesy'.

But back to tonight's meeting. It started with a row. The last meeting in September was the one that Peter Killeen attended in order to agree upon the reselection timetable and start the reselection process. Immediately he left, Tony Mulhearn addressed the meeting. He'd been invited all right, but not in an open and forthright manner. They asked for permission to invite 'a speaker from Liverpool Council that could explain Liverpool's case'. We knew, and they knew, that the speaker would be Tony Mulhearn, but they never said so openly. They even have to be devious when they've got enough votes to insist anyway.

Before Mulhearn spoke several members objected to his addressing the meeting on the grounds that the reselection procedure had now started, that he was a declared runner, and that he would, therefore, be guilty of breaking the rules and canvassing. They were right, but that didn't matter. They were outvoted and Tony Mulhearn was allowed to make his speech.

However, the Minutes of the meeting that they were asked to approve tonight as a 'true and accurate record' of the September meeting contained no reference to these objections. The member who had made the original challenge to Mulhearn, Dave Brown, now a mature student on a trade union scholarship at Ruskin College, Oxford, pointed out the omission and asked for it to be corrected.

'No,' the chairman said. 'We don't have to put everything in the minutes.' He made to move onto the next piece of business.

'But this is important,' Dave Brown persisted from the back of the small former classroom. He stood up. 'I'd like them corrected, please. Otherwise they're not a true and accurate record.'

82

'Yes, they are,' the Militant chairman insisted with the vocal support of his acolytes.

The delegate stood again. 'I'm sorry, chairman, but they can't be,' he said politely.

'Sit down,' they screamed at him. 'Sit down, you dickhead,' screeched one sitting near me at the front of the room. Dave bravely stood his ground. 'If you don't sit down,' the chairman threatened, also standing, 'I'll have you thrown out.'

There was uproar. Those who wanted the minutes corrected were assailed by torrents of abuse and screamed at by the secretary; the hulabaloo culminated in one of the more elderly members being asked to step outside.

'Put it to the vote,' the Militants kept chanting, 'Put it to the vote.' And they did. They voted that the minutes of the last meeting were a 'true and accurate record' of that meeting even though they had all acknowledged that they were not.

At any other time, in any other party, anywhere, the minutes would have been corrected. Why make a fuss? If there's a mistake or something missing, and someone wants it put right, even if it's only a trivial matter, then you do it, if only to keep them quiet. It's quickest and easiest, and it's the proper way to dispose of the matter. But not here. They display an arrogance and totalitarianism that's frightening.

The row lasted for ten or fifteen minutes, although that was just the beginning. Worse followed. Frances Bailey, a long-standing stalwart of the party, courageously moved a resolution from the women's council, congratulating Neil on the initiative that he had taken against the Militants at the Conference. She was shouted at, laughed at and generally heckled – they actually hooted. The resolution was defeated.

Not so the resolution moved by one of the delegates recently taken into the employ of Liverpool Council and a delegate from the Militant-dominated Liverpool GMBATU Branch 5, a resolution which condemned Neil Kinnock for his 'unprovoked and unjustified' attack on the workforce and the people of Merseyside. It referred, of course, to his speech attacking the Militants.

In moving the resolution the proposer called the leader of the Labour party a 'liar', a 'cheat', a 'traitor' and a 'rat'. The words, like his entire speech, were delivered with vehemence and spite. His reward was prolonged and loud applause and the stamping of feet on the ground. They were all smiling. They all seemed to be enjoying the pantomime. They were asserting themselves and it obviously felt good. The resolution was passed by an overwhelming majority to sustained cheering, while the small group of 'real' Labour party members at the back of the room looked glum and defeated.

At that point, I rose to give my parliamentary report. I stood where I had been sitting, at the front of the room, alongside the secretary and the chairman.

'Before I give my parliamentary report,' I started, 'I want to comment on what has just been said about the leader of the Labour party . . .'

'Point of order, point of order.' Several Militants immediately jumped to their feet, their arms raised, competing with each other for the attention of the chairman. Indeed, they were competing with him, as he also stood up shouting, 'Point of order. Point of order.' I don't think that I've ever seen the chairman of a meeting get up and address a point of order to himself before. At least that gave the members of the 'real' Labour party something to smile at.

I sat down again. I felt absolutely calm and determined. No matter how long it took, how much they shouted, I was going to tell the truth.

'Just tell us what you've been doing in Parliament,' the chairman insisted. 'That's all you're entitled to do.'

'I will,' I said, as I stood up again, 'when I've dealt with the lies that have . . .'

There must have been a dozen of them standing this time, all screaming, faces twisted and distorted, among them Lawler and Kerr just inches away from me in the front row. I waited for them to resume their seats and for the noise to subside.

I stood again. 'I'm reporting on my work in Parliament,' I said quietly and deliberately. 'Part of that is also to report on the performance of the party and of the leader. Now, whatever Neil Kinnock said at the Conference . . .'

I couldn't even hear my own words that time. The disruption lasted for all of twenty minutes. Each time I stood up I continued exactly where I had left off. Eventually the chairman said, 'All right, let him say it. Let's get on with it.'

They then made to leave. They stood and noisily moved the clanking chairs. He motioned for them to stay. Perhaps they were, after all, trying to behave. So I corrected the lies and distortions and supported what Neil had said about the Liverpool Militants. This time the members of the 'real' Labour party were smiling and it was the revolutionaries who looked glum.

Then, when I'd finished defending Neil, I gave my parliamentary report. I'd intended to speak about Norman Fowler's proposed cuts in social security but, while on my feet, I decided to talk about the proposed Public Order Bill, and the new and dangerous offence of 'disorderly conduct' that was being created. I swear that not one of them saw the connection between what I was saying and the way that they behaved. That's the other problem; they have no sense of humour.

Or perhaps they have. Perhaps that's the charitable construction to place on Mulhearn's statement after Neil met the Liverpool councillors in Liverpool yesterday, that Neil had undergone a 'miraculous transformation' and, I think I remember the words accurately, now 'fully supported the campaign'.

That's typical of their manipulation and news management. Neil had to go on Channel 4 News to challenge the version of the meeting being put about by the Militants, which made it look as if he had capitulated and conceded the integrity of their case.

At least they've agreed to withdraw the redundancy notices and to work with a joint Labour party and national trade union initiative to attempt to bridge the £25m gap in the Council's revenue. If this fails they will, apparently, be bankrupt within three weeks. Despite the signs of hope, I don't trust them. They'll either find a way of reneging on an agreement that makes them look like failures, or contrive to put the blame on others. In fact, I'm not all that sure that they should be helped to find a solution. They should be left to hang. They won't be grateful for the help: they will turn on those that help them.

At least it's comforting to know that the Liverpool Militants haven't conned everyone on Merseyside into their way of thinking. An anti-Militant rally at Pier Head on Sunday is said to have attracted 10,000 supporters. Even if the majority were probably Liberals and Tories, at least they're being opposed by the ordinary people. That can't be bad.

Neil is also determined to beat them. I went to see him in his room in the House of Commons this morning, at his request, about my resignation. He was very relaxed. He lounged in a deep armchair opposite me as I sat on its matching sofa. I could see the Thames running past outside the windows. He didn't argue with me, as he

85

had done before. He accepted my decision. Perhaps he was glad. As I've said, it must be embarrassing for him to have a Front Bench spokesman in such constituency difficulties. Neil did ask me not to say anything about resigning until after the Shadow Cabinet elections and the reshuffle of the jobs at the end of the month. He would then add a note to the press release announcing the changes to the effect that I was resigning because I wanted to spend more time on constituency matters.

I agreed. It doesn't matter to me how or when the announcement is made. I don't particularly want it to be publicised. I would be happy for it to pass unnoticed. I certainly don't want to create difficulties either for Neil or the party. Indeed, as I told him, I'm prepared to leave both the timing and the reason for my resignation to him.

We talked about Liverpool and Militant. I stressed how important it is that he should be seen to be in charge; he'll only gain by being seen to be tough with them. We talked about my problem too. I told him that I was going to go down fighting.

'Keep fighting, kid,' he said, as I left.

Earlier today, before all this, Jan took Chloe to the vet to have her put down. She and Natasha both cried, and Natasha was particularly upset, even though we had agreed that Chloe was in pain and distress and that it was unavoidable. I felt guilty as I left them to drive to London, knowing I would not be back home until sometime late on Wednesday evening. I never seem to be able to be at home when I'm needed. I just hope that that's not what they feel too.

Wednesday 23rd October 1985

Reading the newspaper on the plane to London from Manchester this morning, my eyes – for some reason – lifted to the date. 'Wednesday 23rd October,' *The Times* recorded. It was on this date, over forty years ago, that my father, William Silk, was killed when his ship, the *Charybdis*, was torpedoed in the Channel by a German submarine. It seems a terribly long time ago. My mother and his sister still speak of him as a young man and as if the episodes that they describe happened only yesterday. He was only a little older when he was killed than my son Dominic, his only grandson, is now.

It made me very sad. The sadness remained with me all day. It hovered over me as I drove from Heathrow to Westminster, as I struggled with a mountain of letters and telephone messages that Sarah had left in the small office on the Upper Committee corridor (North) that I share with Tony Lloyd, the Member for Stretford, and it accompanied me to a pork pie and pickled onion lunch in the gloom of the Tea Room.

By the time I voted at seven o'clock on the Government's refusal to impose sanctions on South Africa and then again at ten o'clock, this time for an independent judicial inquiry into the Handsworth riot, I was thoroughly depressed. No doubt a great deal of this is attributable to tiredness. It has been a long two days. We do work silly hours. It is also, of course, a hangover from the bitterness of the meeting in the constituency, which would sadden and depress anyone.

But I was thinking a great deal about my father and stepfather, both dead. After the death of my father in the war my mother married his best friend, John Kilroy, who had competed with my father for her favours when they were all still at school in the slums of Birmingham. She ended up marrying them both. She loved my stepfather, and it was a very happy marriage. As far as I was concerned, he *was* my father; I've known no other. He treated me and his daughter, my half-sister Madeline, scrupulously fairly. He wanted me for his son, and thought of me as such, yet was always insistent on my fulfilling my duty and visiting my own father's widowed mother after mass on Sundays.

I was very lucky. I had two close and loving families – the Kilroys and the Silks – as well as my mother's, the O'Rourkes. I also had two surnames. At home and in the neighbourhood I was Robert Kilroy, but at school I was Robert Silk, the name on my birth certificate. My stepfather always refused to adopt me or to change my name legally. 'He's Billy's lad,' he'd say. 'He'll stay Billy's lad. But I'll bring him up as mine.'

It used to cause me a great deal of embarrassment that I was always having to explain why I had different names. But it was nothing compared to the anguish that I experienced in my early teens when I had to decide what to call myself, for whatever name I chose would disappoint one family, though they would never say so. There was no way that I could renege on my own name and father, but neither did I want to hurt my stepfather. It was my headmaster who suggested the simple expedient of putting the Kilroy before the

Silk, but without the hyphen. Some editor or printer at LSE when I worked for the college newspaper, *Beaver*, put that in, and it stayed.

My stepfather was a good man. He died of a heart attack at the early age of 53 just a few days after I was first elected. It was probably the excitement of seeing me elected that killed him, though the stress of his time as the rear gunner in a Lancaster bomber also helped.

I miss my stepfather, especially as my own children have never really had the luxury of a grandfather – Jan's dad also died in his early fifties – but it is my mother that I really feel sorry for. She's had a romantic and yet sad life. She misses my stepfather and is very lonely.

Thinking about all this, becoming more depressed in the process, put the Militants in Knowsley in context. They're trivial and unimportant.

Thursday 24th October 1985

Home Office Question Time today, and I stayed at home. It must be the first time that I have not been in the House asking questions when the Home Secretary is up for questioning. The reason I stayed away is, of course, because I have resigned as Shadow Home Office Minister but it has not yet been made public. I couldn't, therefore, be in the Chamber and on the backbenches asking questions – that would have caused comment and speculation and would have needed an explanation – nor, having resigned, could I properly sit on the Front Bench.

It was at least a good excuse to stay at home and catch up with the constituency correspondence and the long list of individual cases, especially as there was no vote tonight. The letters and the phone calls that have to be made quickly accumulate if you're away from Parliament for a day, as I was when in the constituency on Tuesday for that awful meeting, even though Sarah and Noni do their best to lighten the load.

One of the most interesting, if also the most time-consuming, cases was the claim brought to me by one of my parish councillors in Prescot, Jean Whitehead. She claims that there are more deaths from heart attacks in Prescot than there ought to be and wonders if the discharge from the BICC factory is to blame. I've written to the

Health Minister for the figures on heart deaths for the areas, as well as to the Health and Safety Executive. I'm sure she's right.

I feel quite ill myself. I also feel inordinately tired when I return home from the constituency, especially if I've driven. It's so bad that I often walk around the next day feeling drugged. It's difficult, in these circumstances, to get any real work done. The tiredness is attributable in part to the fact that when I'm in the constituency I frequently go to bed late after a long day. Usually I'm in the RAF club or the BUFF club in Kirkby with Geoff and Frances Kneale or, on Fridays, in the Prescot Labour Club after a long surgery at each of the four main centres in the constituency. Then, if it's a weekday, I get up early to catch the British Airways Super Shuttle (and it is super) to Heathrow, and from there travel by car to Westminster before returning home, if I'm lucky, before eleven and in time to watch *Newsnight*. But the tiredness the day after is not just due to the shortage of sleep, exacerbated by being in a strange bed. It's also the nervous energy that I expend. There are times when I suddenly become aware of how tense I am, how tightly my fists are clenched. It was like that on Tuesday.

At least I haven't upset Michael Cockerell. I was talking to him on the phone and promising to send him some of the documents I've got from my source in the T & G that he wants for his film, which is to be screened this coming Sunday morning. As we were speaking I started to write out the envelope.

'How do you spell your name?' I asked.

'The same as you did in the *New Statesman*,' he answered.

I was amazed. I didn't remember ever writing about him, still less in the *New Statesman*. What had I said? Was it bad? Did he still hold it against me? Would it show in his treatment of my story in the film?

'I've never written about you,' I said, still trying to remember.

'Yes, you have. In the diary. You wrote about being at Tom Bower's party to launch his book on Claus Barbie.'

So I had, but I still didn't remember mentioning Cockerell, or even seeing him there. If I had written about him, and in a diary, there is a good chance that it wouldn't be complimentary. I checked by files as soon as I got home. It's all right, I merely said that he was also at the party. Thank God for that. That's one enemy I haven't made.

I'm going to have to make an enemy of David Mellor, the junior Home Office Minister. Admittedly it will not be very difficult; many of his own colleagues seem to have achieved that state with ease. My reason is that he keeps insisting that Leon Brittan's promise to me to end the routine use of police and court cells to hold unconvicted and unsentenced persons has been fulfilled. Yet Parliamentary answers from him to me today show that these cells have been used most nights so far this year. Moreover, there was one night in September, ten nights in August, and three consecutive nights in July when more than a hundred people were being held.

It would have been better for us all if David Mellor had acknowledged the truth of the problem and set out the measures he proposes to deal with it. After all, it was Leon Brittan who, as Home Secretary, said that the 'practice is highly undesirable'. He went further. 'Police cells,' he said, 'were not built to hold such prisoners. Their use causes hardship, both to the prisoners and to their visitors, especially lawyers.'

It's the physical conditions that cause the most concern. Most cells are below ground level, have no natural light and hold two or more people, often with their mattresses adjoining each other on the floor. The prisoners have no access to adequate washing or bathing facilities and no proper access to work, educational or recreational facilities. As I saw when I visited them, they are required to speak to their visitors and lawyers through a narrow slit in the metal cell door. Nor are they held in these degrading and humiliating conditions for a short period of time – many will be detained for several nights, if not weeks. The longest period of dentention in 1984 was 36 nights and so far this year, as Mellor acknowledges, 29 nights.

This cannot be allowed to continue, but it will if the minister insists on being blind to the problem. There is certainly no public fuss, no outcry, no press, no demonstrations in the street about this matter, nor will there be. I shall have to mobilise the Penal Affairs Group to raise the issue again, to get some publicity and put pressure on the Government. As a beginning I made sure that *Police Review* carried the figures as a news item.

Being at home meant that we could have a family conference about getting a dog. We all agree that we should have one. Jan and I want another yellow labrador called Chloe, like the last one. She would be the third we have had. Both of the others had cancer well before they reached the age of ten. Natasha wants a labrador but said it should be black and should be called Paddy. That, strangely, was what my Grandmother Silk had, although Natasha did not know that. Dominic wants a Weimaraner. With fifty per cent of the votes between us, Jan and I couldn't lose. Although Dominic vigorously dissented, we eventually agreed that we will get a labrador, but we'll decide between black and yellow at the time of choosing and the name will be determined later. I think Jan and I will win.

Friday 25th and Saturday 26th October 1985

How could I have forgotten? At the management committee meeting on Tuesday evening the constituency secretary, Cathy Toner, admitted, when dealing with the correspondence, that she had received a letter earlier in the year and again this month from the secretary of the Liverpool North Branch of TASS seeking affiliation to the constituency and that she had refused him affiliation. I like the way she does these things so cavalierly, without informing anyone – or at least without informing the management committee.

I was also sent copies of the correspondence by the TASS secretary. He first wrote on 18th March 1985 asking for affiliation and nomination papers for the Parliamentary candidature when they became available, but made the mistake of saying, in effect, that the branch would support me. His letter was ignored. According to the minutes of the June meeting of his union branch they again wrote, this time to the assistant secretary, seeking affiliation to the constituency. They applied again, this time by recorded delivery to the secretary, with a copy to me, on 15th October 1985. This was the letter the constituency secretary referred to. She acknowledged receipt and then added tartly, 'but I've turned them down because he [the TASS branch secretary] doesn't live in the constituency'. True enough – but this, as she must know, is not a reason for refusing to allow his branch to affiliate. If it is then why, one wonders, didn't she refuse the affiliation of all the T & G branches whose secretaries do not live in the constituency? There are plenty who do not, especially of those newly affiliated. That she made a mistake is not in doubt; that it was a deliberate one is more than likely. I've told Geoff Kneale and Peter Fisher. It will go into our files and be reported to Peter Killeen as yet more evidence of strange doings.

These are not the only strange events. The Liverpool Militants are now saying, in the press, that they've got a tape of Neil at the meeting where he's supposed to have had a miraculous conversion and supported their campaign. If they have it, I wonder why they don't produce it? On the other hand, why say there's one if there isn't? Or is it all designed to cause confusion? It it's the latter then they're succeeding.

On Fridays the House of Commons has a distinctive atmosphere and a totally different character to that of any other day. It's quieter and more relaxed, almost civilised. This is, of course, because there are relatively few MPs around. No committees sit on Fridays and there are usually no votes. The session itself only lasts from 9.30 am to 2.30 pm, and, because the day is normally given over to back-benchers or non-controversial Government business, there tends to be a co-operative, almost academic atmosphere in the chamber. It's even friendly. It's certainly a far cry from the hustle and the bustle and the noise and shouting and conflict that characterise a normal day.

I called in to collect some papers from my office and to deal with some constituency cases. One of those concerned a lady who had been given an appointment for a year's time to attend the Pain Relief Clinic at Walton Hospital. As you would expect, that made her both angry and distressed — when I saw her she was in considerable pain. And the Prime Minister has the cheek to say that the National Health Service is safe in her hands and that her Government is providing more resources for it.

I also collected an answer to a parliamentary question that I had tabled about the working of the new Repatriation of Prisoners Act. This enables prisoners in the participating countries to be transferred to their own country to serve out their sentences. So far no British prisoners held in custody abroad have been repatriated to Britain. There are, however, 19 applications for repatriation from foreigners in British prisons. The Home Office estimates that there are 77 foreign prisoners eligible for transfer. I'm concerned to ensure that they are transferred if that is what they want. I'm even more anxious to ensure that as many British subjects as possible can serve out their sentences in Britain, if only for the sake of their families who would then be able to visit them. Punish the offender, yes, but there is no need also to punish their relatives unnecessarily by denying them the chance to make visits to the offenders.

When I spoke to Jan on the phone later on Friday evening from Kirkby, she was more concerned about repatriating Natasha from Slough. Natasha went there with several friends to a concert featuring The Cult and was to return by train and stay at a friend's house. Naturally, she's refused Jan's offer to collect them all, so Jan was fretting about the safety of our sixteen-year-old daughter. I reassured her. 'Don't worry,' I said, 'she'll be all right.' And then I worried and couldn't get to sleep.

The *Punch* lunch that I attended at the magazine's plush offices in Tudor Street on Friday, before leaving for the constituency, seemed to be a whole world away from Liverpool and the Militants, though both were mentioned. It was an absolute riot of a lunch, noisy and boozy. Alan Coren, the master of ceremonies, was no noisier than Melvyn Bragg on his left and me on his right, though he was considerably funnier than either of us. I can't remember the last time that I have relaxed and laughed so much as I did yesterday. Of course, the presence of so many cartoonists and genuinely witty people does help to create a special kind of atmosphere. Then I thought of the political problems of my future, and I became gloomy.

Beating Luton on Saturday helped to lessen the gloom. The consoling thing about Manchester United's victory and the fact that we're still ten points adrift in the league is that they beat Chelsea. Two southern teams beaten by two northern teams is a good way to end a Saturday spent in a cold and wet garden planting bulbs.

I've put in dozens. A whole sackful. Some are crocuses to add to the scatter of yellow and white that we already get beneath the high beech tree, the rest are the full white daffodils that Jan likes and that I planted in abundance in a new flower bed that we've dug out of the lawn directly opposite the kitchen window. The remainder, and there are a lot in a sack, have been put along the drive under the pines and the laurels. If they flower there they'll look very good, but I'm afraid that I've wasted my time. The ground is nearly always dry there, sheltered as it is by the tall old pines where magpies and collard doves nest. The bulbs probably won't get enough moisture, even though I've put them in extra deep. And, if they do survive, I must make sure that the ducks don't walk all over them or the geese bite off the new shoots, which is what happened last year. We let the geese and ducks out to roam the whole garden because they seemed to be short of food. They had a great time. The only trouble was that the ducks shovelled up all my favourite and carefully nurtured sweet williams, and the geese ate the tender new shoots of the delphiniums that I'd grown from seed two years ago.

As I moved from one part of the garden to another I felt that there was something wrong, something missing. It was the dog. She would usually have followed close at my heels and waited patiently as I dug the holes to put in the bulbs. I miss her.

Natasha is also miserable. One of her friends, fortunately not a close one, has been killed in a motorbike accident. It made Jan and me shudder. We've strenuously resisted all entreaties from Dominic to let him have one and given him the use of our cars as recompense. It's caused many family rows, and there have been even more when he occasionally turns up on the back of a friend's or even, on one occasion, borrowed one so that he could go back and forth to work during the summer at a petrol station.

'But you can borrow my car,' I said, grandiloquently.

'It's not such good fun,' he answered.

That's what we're worried about, although I didn't say so.

Sunday 27th October 1985

The big film. I was nervous about it, concerned about how I would be portrayed. So was Jan. We've never been like this before for any of the numerous television programmes that I've been on. But then this is different, it's not just an ordinary interview or debate.

The film itself left me slightly disappointed. It was fair enough, and it was on my side. There was no doubt about that. It spoke of the 'bloody battle' for Knowsley North and accurately presented my views and allegations. But unfortunately it also said, or rather Michael Cockerell did, that I would fight a by-election if deselected. We played the film back again, and nowhere did I say that. It was his assumption, but it will cause me trouble.

Frances Bailey and the other women in Knowsley came over well. Edna talked of how coming to Labour party meetings used to be a pleasure, but wasn't any more. 'They bawl,' she said. 'They ought to form their own party, they're splitting ours.' Muriel Marsden, the wife of Frank, the former MP for Liverpool, Scotland Exchange, who is also on my management committee, told how the Militants 'forced their opinions down everyone else's throat and voted en bloc'.

There were some surprises, too. They had filmed Mulhearn entering the Municipal Annex in Liverpool – and who should be guarding the entrance in his role of recently recruited security officer but Joe Lawler, the man we now know is not even a delegate. They interviewed him. What the film crew and Cockerell did not know, however, was that the same shot also showed yet another of my councillors, a member of the management committee, a Militant supporter and an employee in the security force, Tony Rainford.

Peter Fisher was impressive. He sounded honest and sincere, as he is. He spoke of the use of patronage and of the number of Militant supporters on my management committee who work for Liverpool City Council. Much more interesting, however, was Hatton's reaction to all this.

'You could count the number of people on Knowsley North on one hand,' he said to Michael Cockerell, 'and still have a couple of fingers to spare.' He was talking about the number of delegates on my management committee who worked for Liverpool City Council. But how does he know? Why should he know? The fact that he even knows that some of his new employees are on my mangement committee is interesting in itself. He's obviously made it his business to know. I bet he doesn't know how many there are on the Labour management committees in Tory seats. I think he scored an own goal there.

The local Militants were also in evidence in the film: Jim McGinley denying everything and conning no-one, not even, I suspect, himself; two more from the Kirkby Unemployed Centre, one calling for a Militant candidate with a 'large M', and the other saying that I had done nothing for the constituency. But Cockerell faithfully reported the packing of meetings, the influence of Militant and its base in Liverpool and that national party officials had described what was happening in my constituency as a 'scandal', I did not know that.

The surprise was the discussion that took place in the studio afterwards with Frank Field and Jeremy Corbyn, the hard left MP for Islington North. I wasn't told this would happen. Frank was all right, though I wish he'd been tougher and more forceful.

Does this, David Dimbleby asked him, have echoes for you? 'Echoes?' Frank said, 'They're the same characters.' And so, of course, they are – those that tried and failed to unseat Frank are now at work in Knowsley. He added that he had had a 'civil war for three years', that it had totally occupied his energies and that many other

95

MPs had taken early retirement rather than face what he went through and I am now experiencing.

I'd forgotten that, but it's true. They tend to get ignored. Lots of our colleagues who would have wanted to continue at least for another Parliament have chucked in the towel rather than face a nasty reselection battle and the prospect of being beaten.

Jeremy Corbyn was the one who made me blaze. Oh, he declared, nothing to worry about here. All got up by the media. It's the media, the ex-public schoolboy said, that's created all this, they've created the 'conflict', the 'division', the 'strife'. The bastard, he even cast doubts both on Cockerell's integrity and, more important, on the Knowsley women's credibility by suggesting that the reporter had 'looked long' to get that kind of quote. He hadn't looked at all. The comments had been thrust at him by decent Labour women.

Remembering how afraid those women had been, how Edna hasn't been able to sleep at night after the interview and had asked for her contribution to be cut out, I can't wait to give him an example of the healthy debate he thinks is being conducted in Knowsley.

I can't understand why he said it. He doesn't know anything about my constituency, he's never asked me about it and has never, as far as I am aware, visited it. Yet there he was 200 miles away in the warmth and security of the television studios pontificating at great length about it and me. He didn't even have the decency, the courtesy to let me know in advance that he would be appearing on the programme specifically to talk about my reselection. Thank God David Dimbleby was there. He was good. 'They're weasel words,' he said to Corbyn.

That apart, we decided it would do. Mum, who rang immediately, liked it; so did Jan's mother. Sam Silkin, the former Attorney General MP for Dulwich, also rang. He wanted to encourage me. No-one else phoned, except Michael Cockerell. He is obviously delighted and expected me to be. I'm too close. It's too important. I can't be objective.

We walked in the woods, which didn't seem the same without the dog. We decided that the film was okay. We can live with it. But I've still got to see Corbyn. Jan is angry with him, but more worried about what I'll do to him.

Monday 28th October 1985

We've got another one. Dave Kerr, a Militant supporter, an employee of Liverpool City Council and press officer of the constituency party, is not, according to the Tobacco Works' Union, a delegate. Yet that's how he's listed on the list of delegates that the secretary has prepared for Peter Killeen.

It really is extraordinary how two of the noisiest and most active of the delegates, who always sit in the front row and who are experts at hurling abuse are not even entitled to be at the meetings, let alone play any part in them, according to the union they say has sent them. I don't understand how it is that the secretary doesn't know all this. After all, she was very quick to tell the TASS man to get lost. Why hasn't she ever noticed that Lawler and Kerr have not been nominated by the unions they claim to have been nominated by?

Like the removal of Lawler it doesn't make a great deal of difference to the vote. There are now 140 delegates, I still need 71 votes to win and I still have 66 with another ten possibles. We're making progress, although there's a long way to go. But as with the elimination of Lawler, it's a morale boost for me and, more importantly, for Peter Fisher, who has done all the work and challenged their right to attend the selection conference. It will also raise the spirits of all those who only a few days ago were threatening to leave and hold their own meetings. They will like their suspicions that dirty and underhand work is being done to be confirmed in such a way, and it once again raises important questions about the constitutional propriety and the validity of all the meetings these 'delegates' have both attended and at which they have voted.

Before all this I read Michael Cockerell's feature article in *The Times*, grandly entitled 'Who Will Win the Merseyside Showdown?', which says that 'there is considerable evidence of an organised attempt by Militants to take over' Knowsley North. More reassuringly, he says – and I know that he has talked to a lot of people off the record – that the Labour Party north-west regional headquarters is carrying out full-scale investigations into the credentials of all 142 delegates, that it has 'discovered irregularities', and that it is determined that the selection procedure will be 100 per cent above board. Nevertheless, he concludes, 'the campaign to unseat

Kilroy-Silk demonstrates that on Merseyside, at least, the Tendency tacticians are still alive and at work.' Don't I know it.

I was surprised by the prominence given to the article, as well as by the press enquiries following the programme on Sunday and the comments of people that I've spoken to. There is a good deal more interest in my saga than I expected there to be. I decided to use Cockerell's article as a peg to keep the pot boiling. As Jan said, there is no point in being a shrinking violet – not that I've been accused of that very often.

I wrote a letter to *The Times* saying that Michael Cockerell's account of the reselection battle in Knowsley North could not be expected to convey an adequate flavour of constituency party meetings dominated by members of the Militant Tendency. I gave a brief account of the last meeting, and I ended it by getting a dig in at that rat Jeremy Corbyn and his description in the programme of what is happening at my meetings as being 'healthy debate'.

Rather surprisingly, I also managed to distance myself enough to draft an article on women and babies in prison, based on the replies that I received today to some parliamentary questions that I tabled. These show that on the latest available date, 18th October 1985, 23 women had their children with them in prison. Six of these are in Holloway prison. Their children's ages range from seven days to 26 weeks. Six women are in Styal, with children whose ages range from two to five and a half months, and eleven women are in Askham Grange, with children aged from three weeks to 15½ months.

I don't think women who have young children to care for should be in prison, unless there are powerful and compelling reasons for their incarceration. I certainly do not believe that it was necessary to send all the 136 girls known to be pregnant to Youth Custody Centres (which used to be called Borstals) in 1984 and for 16 of them to have given birth in custody, especially when one of them had only two weeks of her sentence left to serve, two of them had one month left and five had six weeks to complete.

The practice of remanding unsentenced mothers of young babies and pregnant women is even more questionable. Many of them are subsequently acquitted or given a non-custodial sentence, yet every one of them will, in effect, have served a prison sentence. Of the 22 unsentenced women who gave birth in custody in 1984, four received non-custodial sentences and two were made subjects of extradition orders.

It would be understandable if they had all been charged with or convicted of serious offences or of violence against the person, but this was not the case. The majority of the women were imprisoned for such things as theft, deception and drug offences. One, with a baby of four and a half months, was sentenced to 28 days for shoplifting. That demonstrates what a punitive society we are. I don't suppose we shall ever really change it, but we must keep trying. If we don't then not only will conditions not improve, they will probably get worse. Someone has to be seen to be interested in what is happening, unpopular though the subject is. I sometimes think that that is my major role as a penal reformer – to be known to be around and watching, and in the process act, hopefully, as a deterrent to more serious abuses.

Tuesday 29th October 1985

I eventually saw Jeremy Corbyn in the division lobby during a vote on the Transport Bill this evening. I'd been looking for him in the Commons all day.

I was talking to Barry Sheerman and John Evans, the MP for St Helen's North, strategically placed near the exit through which all the Labour MPs would have to pass, not far from where Bob Parry had offered me that 'deal' all those months ago.

John Evans could see that I was distracted. 'You're not listening,' he complained in his fine Geordie accent. He jabbed me in the ribs with his elbow.

'I'm looking for Corbyn,' I explained. 'I want a word with him.'

'Oh Christ,' he said.

'You know what it's about?' I said.

'Oh aye, I know what it's about well enough. Look Rob,' he said, 'whatever you do, don't hit him.' That was the last thing that Jan said to me. I was about to tell him that when I saw Corbyn walking towards us with Michael Meacher from the far end of the wide green-carpeted, book-lined corridor.

I strode towards them. 'Remember,' John Evans called from behind, 'don't hit him.'

'Hello mate,' Corbyn said to me.

'Don't you mate me,' I answered.

Meacher disappeared.

'Since when,' I asked, blocking Corbyn's way, 'have you been an expert on my constituency, eh? Since when have you been qualified to pontificate on television about it? So it was all just "healthy debate" was it?' I demanded. 'Well, how do you like some healthy debate?'

I don't remember how long I 'spoke' to him. I do remember that I said all that I wanted to say and that he became aware of my displeasure. The creep.

There must have been upwards of two hundred Labour MPs in the lobby at the time but no-one attempted to intervene and no-one said a word. I learned afterwards that that was because most of them were waiting, hoping for me to hit him. There was, apparently, a great demand for the video of the film afterwards and several showings were provided in the Whips' Office.

Distracted by all this I made the mistake of thinking that we had finished voting, and I came home. I was therefore able to watch the *News at Ten* in my own house, a rare luxury. Then, at the end, Alistair Burnett said that there had been a scuffle between two Labour MPs in the lobby tonight and quoted Corbyn as saying that I was a boxer and he was a runner, so he ran. I couldn't believe it. How could he say that about himself?

Then the phone started to ring. I was surprised. I hadn't really expected it to get out, certainly not so soon, and certainly not to evoke the interest that it seems to have attracted. This time I corroborated the story. If Corbyn is going to go around telling everyone about it, as he seems to have done, then I am determined to get my view across.

Before all this I had, on the advice of some colleagues who were members of the National Executive Committee, made the national agent, David Hughes, aware of some of the things that have been happening in the constituency, especially as they bear on the reselection process. I told him about the officers of the party who were not delegates, of the refusal to admit TASS and of the denial for so long of delegate rights to Phil McSorley. I also made sure that he knows of our allegations about the T & G delegation and of the evidence that we have to back them up. In addition I took the opportunity to tell him about the general disorder and the flouting of the rules at the meetings and the threat of the best people to secede.

I don't necessarily expect him to take action at this stage. Indeed, there's a lot to be said for letting things continue a little longer so that we can obtain more evidence of irregularities. But I did want him to know. I didn't want him coming to me in a few months' time when it was too late and saying, 'If only we'd known.'

He was sympathetic, but unspecific.

The conversations with David Hughes took place after I chaired the fortnightly meeting of the Parliamentary Penal Affairs Group. I've been chairman of the group, which is composed of members of all parties in the Houses of Parliament, since I helped to set it up in 1979. We've produced several well-researched and important reports. These include *Too Many Prisoners*, published in 1980, which made 49 recommendations designed to reduce the prison population and which was followed up a year later with a report entitled *Still Too Many Prisoners. Young Offenders – A Strategy for the Future* was published in 1981 and made recommendations aimed at improving policy and practice concerning young offenders. The influence of these reports is shown by the fact that a considerable number of their recommendations were subsequently incorporated into the 1982 Criminal Justice Act. These included the removal of the penalty of imprisonment for vagrancy and soliciting offences – I moved the amendments – the introduction of stricter and more precise statutory criteria for imposing custody and care orders on young offenders; the requirement that courts should normally be required to consider a social enquiry report before imposing a custodial sentence on a young offender or, indeed, on any offender of any age who has not served a previous custodial sentence; a requirement that legal representation must have been offered before a custodial sentence or care order can be made on a young offender; and a legally aided right of application for bail to the Crown Court for those remanded in custody by magistrates courts.

In addition, *Too Many Prisoners* was the first Parliamentary or official report to recommend the repeal of the 'suspected person' law – better known as the 'sus' law – which was repealed the following year, and the first to recommend the introduction of a time limit on remand in custody awaiting trial – the 110 day rule – which is now being implemented by the Government. *Young Offenders – A Strategy for the Future* was also the first such report to recommend a central funding system for intermediate treatment schemes and for facilities for drug abusers. Both are now centrally funded. Nor is that the end of our success. There have been many more. Our 1983 report, *The Prevention of Crime Among Young People* was followed, among other things, by the Home Secretary's announcement of the establishment of a new Crime Prevention Unit in the Home Office while our report, *New Deal for Victims*, published in 1984, led to the establishment of a number of experimental repatriation schemes in various parts of the country. I don't somehow think that we will have the same degree of success with our report on *Life Sentence Prisoners* which we are just about to publish.

It recommends, among other things, that a life sentence should be the maximim, rather than the mandatory sentence for murder; that a number of small units of no more than 40 prisoners should be established for the growing number of life-sentence prisoners and that Leon Brittan's disgraceful and reactionary policy of refusing release on licence for at least 20 years for certain categories of life-sentence prisoners should be discontinued.

Tonight, the meeting in the splendid and ornate Jubilee Room near the part of Westminster Hall where the IRA bomb exploded in 1974 was as usual well attended. It was also, as always, dominated by members from the Lords. They're lucky. They don't have constituents to worry about, or votes to garner, so they can afford to prosecute unpopular but important causes. Tonight's batch included the hardworking and committed regulars who are the backbone of the Group; the Lords Hunt, Hutchinson, Donaldson and Longford and the Baronesses David, Faithful and Masham. Together with the Bishop of Rochester, who usually drops in, the former Attorny-General, Sam Silkin, now Lord Silkin of Dulwich, and Lords Avebury and Harris, we can muster several ex-chairmen of the parole board, many ex-ministers, an ex-director of social services and a great deal of knowledge and experience in the criminal justice field. This is supplemented by the fact that representatives from the prison officers, the governors, the probation services and from social workers, magistrates and justice clerks, as well as from organisations like the Howard League for Penal Reform, Radical Alternatives to Prison, and the National Association of Victim Support Schemes, also attend on a regular basis. Indeed, it is the only forum where such diverse but inter-related interests sit down together. We've come a long way from one of our first meetings when representatives of the prison officers would not sit in the same room as representatives of the prison governors. I had to see them separately and eventually placated them sufficiently so that they became important and constructive contributors to the work of the group.

Most of the agenda is, in fact, set by these various organisations. They come to us with their problems, seeking our support and parliamentary action. Their case has to be good as they know that they are speaking not just to parliamentarians who know their subject, but also in front of their colleagues in the field who may be affected by what they want. Tonight was a case in point. The item on the allegation about bullying in Youth Custody Centres and another critical of the regime at Send Detention Centre had to stand up to the criticism of the prison officers. As you would expect, it makes for sharp but well-informed debate. It also means that these organisations and individuals, who would normally shout at each other from afar via press releases, have to argue their case in a more personal and civilised arena.

We went on to discuss the power of the courts to impose orders on offenders found not guilty by reason of insanity, the qualification of court clerks, the proposed closure of prison workshops – which incidentally aroused a great deal of anger – and the effect of prison on prisoners' families. On all of these matters I was instructed to write to the Home Secretary, Douglas Hurd, expressing our viewpoint. We also agreed that at our next meeting we should discuss the record prison population, that the Home Secretary should be invited to address a meeting of the Group early in the New Year on the prison population and the disturbing increase in the number of remand prisoners.

All this will mean a great deal of extra work for me but most of it will fall on Paul Cavadino, our part-time clerk. He has already, on my instructions, thoroughly researched each item on the agenda and presented us with a paper on it outlining the possible courses of action. He will now draft the letters for me to sign as well as preparing the papers for the next meeting in two weeks' time. We would not be nearly so successful and effective if we did not have him working for us, courtesy of a grant of £36,000 that I managed to obtain from the Cadbury Trust for the lifetime of the Parliament.

As I sat at the head of the large brown leather-topped table in this spacious and beautiful room, with its six chandeliers, its oak panels and its ticking clock, listening to my colleagues making their points with the exaggerated courtesy and grace that seems to be an inevitable feature of all-party groups and committees, I couldn't avoid thinking about my reselection problems. At least if I am deselected I will have the consolation of having brought about some reforms in this otherwise unpopular and neglected field, not the least of which is the ending of the barbaric and indefensible practice of remanding fourteen- to sixteen-year-old schoolchildren in adult prisons. It has taken me ten years to end that blight on our criminal justice system. Not, of course, that I will be remembered for it, or anything else, but that doesn't really matter.

I came away from the meeting satisfied with a job well done. I had not felt that when I left the Chamber of the House two hours earlier, after Question Time. It didn't surprise or particularly disappoint me that I failed to get called to ask a question of the Prime Minister at this, one of her twice-weekly fifteen-minute stints at the despatch box answering a whole range of questions. The competition is always severe and as I did not have a question of my own high enough up on the Order Paper, I would have been lucky to have been called. I had, however, expected to be called at least once during the preceeding 45 minutes of 'Employment Questions', especially as I have one of the highest levels of unemployment in the country in my constituency.

We're required to put in a written question for oral answer by the Minister on the floor of the House exactly two weeks in advance. The printer shuffles the questions and prints them in the Order Paper. The Speaker then calls the MPs to ask their questions in the order in which they are printed. He calls the MP who has question number one. The minister stands at the despatch box and reads out the answer. The MP then responds by asking a supplementary question. The minister replies. The Speaker then calls other MPs to put further supplementary questions on the same subject. When he decides that there have been enough questions he will move on to question number two and repeat the process. The result is that there are a series of mini debates around each question. Although only nine questions were dealt with today – an unusually small number; fifteen would be more usual – he called a total of thirty-three members.

I wasn't one of them. I tried to get called on the very first question from my neighbour in St Helen's, John Evans, on the number of long-term unemployed today compared with when we were in office in 1979. That the Speaker did not call me then was disappointing but not disheartening. There were other questions I could, I thought, 'catch his eye' for. At the next question, on whether the unemployed were actively seeking work, asked by the Tory David Heathcoat-Amory, I stood up 12 times. Still he didn't 'see' me. I rested during the exchanges on industrial diseases, started by James Lamond, the MP for Oldham Central and Royston, stood again, 14 times, on the request from Bob Litherland of Manchester Central to know the number of currently unemployed in the UK, rested while there was a short debate on trade union political funds and tried again when Central Fife's Jimmy Hamilton kicked off again on youth unemployment. No luck.

'What you done?' Dennis Skinner asked. I was sitting alongside him on the front bench below the gangway. 'Yer must be in his bad books, kid,' he added, smiling.

I don't know about that but I do know that I felt both tired and frustrated. It was a precious hour, if not wasted then certainly without tangible result. But it's often like that. Much worse is to spend all morning, and perhaps even longer, researching and writing a speech and then sit in the chamber from 2.30 in the afternoon until 10.00 at night and fail to be asked to deliver it. That's really galling. Fortunately it has only happened to me once. I was livid. Almost as bad is to make the speech right at the end of the debate when there are only five minutes or so left and a whole day's work and time is wasted in a rushed gabble. But then, that is the House of Commons for you.

At least by actually being there, on what used to be the Tribune Group's bench, I was contributing to our political battle with the SDP. They have attempted to take over the front bench below the gangway – they have nowhere else to sit as a party. They even attend Prayers at the beginning of each day's session and so are enabled to put a 'Prayer Card' inscribed with their name on the back of the bench and thus reserve their seat.

Members like Dennis Skinner and Dennis Canavan have resisted their take-over. They try to ensure that the bench is always full and that there is no room for David Owen or Roy Jenkins. This happened today. Seated from right to left facing the Tories were Dennis Canavan, Kevin Barron, of Rother Valley, John Cartwright of the SDP, who was assumed to be keeping a place for Owen or Jenkins, Dennis Skinner, myself, Brian Sedgemore for Hackney South and Shoreditch, and Ian Mikardo representing Bow and Poplar. We had spread ourselves so as to fill the whole bench.

Suddenly, both Owen and Jenkins appeared at the bar of the Chamber and stood and surveyed the bench, clearly looking for a space in which to sit for Prime Minister's Questions.

'Watch out,' Dennis Skinner said. He takes all this very seriously. Like the rest of us, he expected Cartwright to get up and do a quick exchange with Jenkins and Owen as they had done several times in the past. 'Move up,' Dennis called out. 'Don't give them room.'

Unfortunately, he meant 'spread out', not 'move up'. Instead, everyone moved to the right and Ian Mikardo at the end of the line obligingly moved too. He left a large gap that Owen and Jenkins, to the cheers and jeers of the Tories, slumped into.

'Thank you, Dennis,' Roy Jenkins called sarcastically along the bench. Dennis pretended not to have heard.

The Tory, Tony Beaumont-Dark sitting directly opposite made sure Dennis knew what had happened. 'There'll be a bottle of claret on its way, Dennis,' he boomed as the Speaker called 'Questions to the Prime Minister'. Such is a small part of our life in the 'mother of parliaments'.

Wednesday 30th October 1985

My letter is in *The Times* today. It's the lead letter. There's also a lot of press coverage under such headlines as the *Daily Mirror*'s 'Punch-up MP does it again'; the *Guardian*'s contribution is 'Division of Labour'.

The press accounts, obviously emanating from Corbyn, not only describe the air as 'very thick with four-letter words', but also claim that I was seen to 'draw back my fist' and had to be restrained. It's not true. I didn't draw back my fist and no-one would have wanted to restrain me. The story that Sean Hughes, my neighbour in Knowsley South, told me about the Chief Whip, Michael Cocks, was typical. 'I thought Bob was really going to hit him,' Sean said to Mike. 'There's plenty of time yet,' Mike answered hopefully.

I had to go to Islington to speak tonight. It was a long-standing promise to speak to the Working Mens College in Camden. There must have been at least a dozen in the audience, and not one of them asked me about Corbyn, reselection, or the Liverpool Militants. That was odd. Were they, I wondered, being polite?

Neil has welcomed the package of measures put forward for the rescue of Liverpool by the four local authority treasurers. 'Playing politics with people's jobs must stop,' he said. Not according to Hatton, though – he's quoted as saying that the package is unacceptable. I knew that whatever the national leadership or their effective nominees came up with he and the Militants would find reasons to rubbish.

Parliament was prorogued today. We shall meet again for the State Opening of the new session on 6th November. These last few days of October have been devoted to clearing up all the business that we did not manage to complete before the summer recess began in August. Anything not dealt with now will not become law and, if the Government wishes to pursue it, will need to go through the whole lengthy parliamentary process again from scratch. Hence the government's determination to ensure that Parliament met for these few October days so that it could push everything through.

It also cleared the decks of parliamentary questions. I've had more answers, this time on the inner city riots. There were no riots during the lifetime of the last Labour Government. There have been ten since 1980, beginning with the one at St Paul's, Bristol in 1980 and culminating with the recent 'disturbance', as it is now interestingly called, at the Broadwater Farm Estate, in Tottenham. Well over fifteen hundred police officers and a hundred civilians have been injured, dozens of buildings destroyed and hundreds of others damaged. And the reason for all this carnage? The junior Home Office Minister, Giles Shaw, told me that they were 'hostility to the police, criminal opportunists and a general alienation from authority in areas with special social problems'. The problem is that the Government, whilst perhaps recognising some of the causes of the riots, is not doing much to deal with them. Indeed, it is adding to the problem by its blatant refusal to tackle the terrible decay of many of our inner cities and outer housing estates, and the increase in unemployment. We shall all pay the price for this.

Thursday 31st October 1985

A fantastic day. All day long the evil-eyed nuthatch hammered away at nuts high in the beech tree. We've identified the place that he lodges them in so we tiptoe across the lawn every time that we hear him at work. We can now get a clear view of him, thanks to the new

Pentax binoculars that Jan has bought me. What's more, the green woodpecker posed like an advert for Bulmer's cider high on the trunk of the pine tree this morning and we saw the greater spotted woodpecker in the laurels in the afternoon. And, when running across the still firm ground of the bare fields this morning, I saw two jays.

I also learned that we would not be having a Weimaraner, although I thought we had already decided that. Jan, without confiding in me, had entertained the idea of getting two dogs, a yellow or black labrador and a Weimaraner. She was trying to placate Dominic. She had rung up a breeder and asked about the temperament of the dog. Would it, Jan had asked, be all right with cats and ducks and geese. 'Oh no,' the woman had replied, 'It will kill them all. And you will need a six foot high chain link fence.'

That settled it. We'll stick to the tried and trusted labrador. Jan's action on this occasion reminded me of the time the three of them, she, Natasha and Dominic went to the cat's refuge to replace our ginger tom, which had been run over, and returned with three ginger cats because they didn't want to separate the two brothers from each other or from their mother. We still have all three.

Meanwhile, the *Sun*, in an editorial, tells me to 'Cool it!' According to the paper I'm an 'able and likeable fellow'. That's nice. But I'm 'also far too hot-tempered'. True.

It then says that I had to be restrained from punching Corbyn and that I was involved in a 'barney' – I like that word, its ages since I've heard it used – at the Conference. Being provoked once, it cautions, is understandable. Twice is too much of a luxury. 'Three times, Robert, and you may be dumped anyway. Better cool it.'

I'm not too sure about that.

What is certain, unfortunately, is that yet more jobs in the constituency will disappear. This time it's the Fazakerley Engineering Works near Kirkby. The management of this Ministry of Defence-owned repair workshops, Williams Motors, have announced its closure following their failure to obtain further Ministry contracts. Although there are not a great many jobs at stake – less than a hundred – it is another blow to the morale of the town and, in some way more important, a loss of the skilled jobs that are rare in this area. There will be no more training apprenticeships available for this type of work.

In order to try to save at least some of the jobs, the workforce had explored the possibility of setting up a workers co-operative and tendering for the contracts themselves. I'd taken a delegation of stewards and managers to meet Lord Trefgarne, the Minister of State for Defence, to see if he would help. He would. He has been more than sympathetic. It was our own people who were difficult. The Merseyside Cooperative Development Agency, funded by the Merseyside County Council and Knowsley and St Helen's Councils, considered it to be 'inappropriate for the agency to assist persons engaged in war-related production'!

Great. I suppose we're expected to ward off potential invaders with broomhandles. At the request of the union, the T & G, I'm making one last plea to the Ministers, but it won't come to anything. His hands are tied by Government policy.

Friday 1st November 1985

Tony Bevins rang early this morning. Had I seen the article in *The Times* written by Peter Davenport? No, not yet. He insisted on reading it out to me even though I told him I was in the bath.

It was all right. It said that national party officials are closely watching the investigation of my management committee, and goes on to quote me accurately and fairly in repudiating the Militant's reiterated complaints that I haven't alleviated the unemployment problem and do not live in the constituency.

'Now we come to the worrying part,' Tony said. I sat up, my shoulders cold. He quoted. 'However, he has his critics in the constituency party. Mr Dave Kerr, its press officer, said: 'The whole situation over the past few months has done nobody any good . . . he has not helped his own case with his outrageous attacks.'

'So?' I queried.

'Well, doesn't that mean you're losing friends?'

'But he's a Militant,' I laughed. 'He's not even a delegate.' I was relieved. Was that all that was wrong?

'But that's terrible,' Tony responded. 'You know that, but Peter Davenport obviously doesn't. Nor did I. I was taken in by it. And if I was,' he said, 'then everyone else will be too.'

He has a point.

I thought that I ought to put the record straight and write a letter to *The Times*, but as it was too late for tomorrow's paper, I decided to deliver it by hand on Saturday evening. I wrote it straight away, while the words were still fresh in my mind.

'The insidious nature of Militant Tendency infiltration of the Labour party,' I wrote, 'is demonstrated by the way in which a well-informed, respected and perceptive reporter like Peter Davenport can be manipulated by them.'

I went on to quote the passage about my having 'critics' and that he cites Dave Kerr as evidence of this, as if Kerr were impartial, whereas he is a well-known supporter of the Militants, an employee of Liverpool City Council, and a constant critic of mine.

Then Jan and I rushed off to Knowsley. We drove to Heathrow, parked the car, boarded the plane ten minutes before it took off and arrived in Manchester forty minutes later. Another half an hour by hired car along the M56, and M6, and M62 and, finally, the M57 and we were in the constituency. We lunched with Peter and Jan Fisher at Lee's Garden Chinese restaurant on the road to Ormskirk, before going to the Women's Royal Voluntary Service's Open Day in Richard Hesketh Drive, Kirkby. Sherry was served as one of the local councillor's wives proudly showed us all the clothes they had collected and carefully stored and labelled for the poor and needy. Not only is there a big demand for this free second-hand clothing, people also attempt, we were told, to subvert the rules in order to get more than their entitlement. What a comment on Mrs Thatcher's Britain!

As we walked into Kirkby town centre, people waved from across the street, stuck their thumbs up, shouted 'Don't let them beat you lad', and similar forms of encouragement. Several stopped us to express support. We received the same reception later that afternoon in Stockbridge Village where I made some house visits. It was tremendous. There were constant comments, both on my boxing ability, of which they seemed to be proud, and of my need to stand up against and to beat the Militants.

'We're not having them here,' was the most often-repeated expression.

I experienced this reaction a couple of weeks ago after the initial burst of publicity about the battle for Knowsley North, but it was the first time that Jan had come across it.

'I think you should stand,' she said as we left the newsagents in Stockbridge Village with a copy of the *Liverpool Echo* and walked back to the Hertz car. 'You'll have no problem. I said you wouldn't. You'll win easily.'

She has always said that. She bases her confidence on her knowledge of the easy, relaxed relationship that I have with my constituents, on the fact that my name is known to them all, that my face is recognisable, and that I'm regarded as a good MP. She thinks that all this can be translated into votes for me in a by-election against a Militant candidate, but I'm doubtful. In the end, when it comes to the crunch, they would support the official Labour candidate – or so I used to think. Now I'm not so sure. I don't think they will, if he's a Militant. Moreover, as Jan says, and Peter Fisher has always insisted, Kilroy-Silk is synonymous with Labour. Many will see my name on the ballot paper and put their cross alongside it as they have always done. Perhaps.

'I think you should do it,' she repeated.

'But we'd have no finance or supporters,' I said, across the roof of the red car as I waited for her to get in from the other side and unlock the door.

'We'd do it on our own,' she said confidently, as she slid into the driving seat. 'The two of us could do it. We could win. It'll be fun. Come on,' she said, putting the car into gear, 'you've nothing to lose.'

Whilst I went the rounds of my regular surgeries in Kirkby, Stockbridge Village, Knowsley Village and, finally, Prescot, Jan attended Rita Kneale's 'At Home' night. She's the daughter of my voluntary agent, Geoff Kneale, and his wife Frances Kneale, the mayor. She's also the girl that attracted most of the attention for her looks and her outspoken comments when the twenty-five young people visited the Prime Minister in Downing Street in March.

Two women at my Kirkby Surgery complained that they could not live on the amount of money that was being allocated to them as social security, and that their families were going without food. One was a young single parent who was worried about the welfare of her two-year-old daughter. The other was an older mother of four children with a disabled and unemployed husband. She could not even afford the fifty pence that the youngest son needed for transport to play football for his youth club. They have all been on social security for some time, so that they've become progressively poorer. Washing machines – if they possess them – carpets, furniture, bedding, clothes and the like, purchased when the husband was in employment, all wear out progressively and do not get replaced.

They not only become poorer, but the gap between their families and even the lowest paid of those in work widens.

What made me really angry, however, were their complaints that they did not have enough food. Only a couple of weeks ago I asked some questions in the House about the amount of food that we, and the rest of the Common Market, destroy each year. I had in mind, naturally, the fact that instead of destroying the food it could be used to prevent people from dying of starvation in places like Ethiopia. Now, it seems, it's needed in order to prevent malnutrition in this country.

The food *is* available. As John Gummer, the junior Minister of Agriculture revealed, in 1983–84 the European Community destroyed 477,207 tonnes of oranges, 382,991 tonnes of apricots, 169,858 tonnes of peaches, 19,482 tonnes of cauliflowers, 4,115 tonnes of tomatoes and much more. In the UK alone, we have in store 57,975 tonnes of bread wheat valued at £7m, 64,742 tonnes of beef valued at £164m, 198,022 tonnes of butter worth £374m and 40,801 tonnes of skimmed milk powder valued at nearly £44m. Last year it cost £46.4m just to store the food.

There is something radically wrong with a society that destroys or stores food on such a scale when much of the world's population is starving and when its own children are going hungry. We must do something about this obscenity. I didn't make the women miserable by telling them all this. Perhaps I should have done. Perhaps that's the only way to generate sufficient pressure for change.

Later, we met up with dozens of supporters in the Prescot Labour Club. It was almost like old times. It could have been Ormskirk. The atmosphere was relaxed and friendly, and they were all keen to carry on the fight. Many of them wanted to know if what was reported in tonight's *Liverpool Echo* was true. It said that a secret list was being drawn up of MPs who would back me if I was deselected and stood as an independent. It quoted Frank Field, who is obviously behind all this, as saying: 'There is a considerable number of MPs who, if Kilroy is deselected, will fight a by-election with him.'

I don't know whether or not there is a secret list. No-one's told me. They haven't even asked me if I want the help. It's Frank. Through me he's fighting the by-election against the Militants that his selection victory deprived him of. He can't wait to take them on and beat them, even if I have to be his proxy. I was flattered, of course, but I also feel that I'm being boxed in. I reminded them that

I've never said I'd fight a by-election. Why should I? I must admit I've never understood the value of having a by-election in such circumstances, especially if you lose, and that is always a possibility. I have no reason to vacate my seat before it is necessary to do so.

Not many of them had seen the even better lead letter in the *Guardian* from Tom Gallagher, a member of the Bradford South Labour party, that appeared under the heading, 'Now is the time for all good Labour members to come to the aid of an embattled MP.' Gallagher, whom as far as I know I have never met, criticised Corbyn for his behaviour on the television programme, for refusing 'to utter one word of support for a colleague fighting off a bid by the Militant Tendency to oust him', and 'for a display of the kind of nastiness that has led thousands of members to give up attending meetings'. He added that Corbyn 'did a bad day's work for the Labour cause on Sunday'. He went on to say that I have my faults, true, but that I am a 'hard-working MP with a long record of campaigning effectively on penal and social issues. He is,' he continued, 'just the kind of MP automatic reselection was designed not to get rid of.'

I agreed with that. I warmed to Tom Gallagher. He seems to be a decent and sensible man even if, as he claims, he's to the left of me. More to the point is that he not only offered to come to Knowsley North to campaign for me if I opt to have a by-election, but he also claimed that a 'similar commitment from hundreds of party members on the left and right would be an even more eloquent gesture than Mr Neil Kinnock's declaration that fanatics shall not prevail inside the party'.

Saturday 2nd and Sunday 3rd November 1985

We hoped to be able to continue the big autumn clear-up and plant-out in the garden this weekend – I also want to spray the gravel drive with weedkiller. If I do it now and then again in the spring, I might just be spared a drive full of weeds. I hate the job of getting them out. Instead, still tired after our return from Knowsley on Saturday afternoon, we drove into London to have dinner with Andrew and Ye Ye Goldman to celebrate his birthday. On the way I delivered my handwritten letter about Dave Kerr to *The Times* office in Gray's Inn Road.

Liverpool won, of course, a Rush goal helping us to beat Leicester 1:0. Manchester United also won. They beat Coventry so we're still second and ten points behind. We barely had time to scan the newspapers on Sunday morning and notice the cartoon of me in boxing kit in Marcia Falkender's column in the *Mail on Sunday* before driving back into London to have lunch with Ruth and Guy, and Guy's boss at Goldcrest, Jake Ebert. The troubles of the company are, as you would expect, preoccupying them both. Everything, it seems, will depend upon the success of their new big films, *Revolution* and *Absolute Beginners*. They have high hopes of both, but in order to bring in the kind of money that is needed they will both have to do well in the United States. Let's hope it works, not just for the good of the British film industry, but for the sake of Guy – who is a great mate – and Jake, who seems a decent, straightforward, no-nonsense bloke, even though a trifle obsessed with tennis. Ruth is having problems too. She wants to entitle the film that she has made for the BBC2 TV *Forty Minutes* programme on the spouses of the Hollywood film moguls *The Real Hollywood Wives*. Jackie Collins, or rather her lawyers, won't let her. Her other film, on Page Three girls, does not seem to be running into any trouble and sounds good.

We'd hardly arrived home in Burnham from lunch when we drove back up the M4 again to Islington to have dinner with an old friend from LSE days and now a Granada TV director, Norma Percy. She has finished a long stint on making the *End of Empire* programme and is now bored and restless with her overlong holiday. Another pleasant evening with her boyfriend, the snail expert Steve Jones, and fellow-guest Mike Elliott, the *Economist*'s lobby man.

I didn't get away either from my own problems or from those of Liverpool during this hectic weekend, of course. Far from it. As if they feel it's a necessary sign of interest and politeness, everyone enquires after my 'problem'. It's a bore.

At least we've sorted out what breed of dog we are going to have, and even selected the puppy. She's a yellow labrador. Natasha, Jan and I drove to the other side of Reading to choose her; we got the pick of the litter. I had forgotten, though, how expensive they are. Dominic refused to accompany us. He wants nothing to do with it. That attitude won't last for long. Jan experienced enormous difficulty in finding one that was for sale. She must have spent a fortune on the phone, with calls to Scotland as well as to Kent and Lancaster.

They've become very popular dogs. It's the Andrex advert apparently.

Monday 4th November 1985

After the hard work of enjoying myself all weekend, I was hoping for a quiet Monday. I wanted to get on top of the constituency correspondence before Parliament reassembled on Tuesday. Some hope.

The phone rang just before seven a.m.

'I have it from an authoritative source,' the breathless Chris Moncrieff, the Press Association's chief political reporter, said, 'that you have resigned from the Front Bench team.'

'That's right,' I said. I was still half asleep. I wondered where he'd got the information, and who this 'authoritative source' was. Who would tell him at seven a.m.? Jan's suggestion that it would probably have been my friend, replacement, and MP for Birmingham Erdington, Robin Corbett, was confirmed later. He put out a press release announcing his own appointment before Neil had issued his statement. That, of course, drew attention to me.

'I don't want to put words into your mouth,' the excited voice continued, 'but is it because of your problems with reselection?'

'Yes.' I felt weary. I'd have to go through the whole bloody story again.

'Would you like to comment?' Chris asked hopefully.

Why not? I thought. There was no point in being bashful. So I heaved myself up to a sitting position, drew breath and commented, at length. I repeated the same story to the subsequent callers from Radio City, Radio Merseyside and Independent Radio News, Andy Grice from the *Liverpool Echo* – who, incidentally, asked the most perceptive and challenging questions of all those who interrogated me today – Philip Webster of *The Times* and Graham Jones of the *Daily Telegraph*. It was the latter who told me of the feature on me in today's *Sun*.

'You're a folk hero,' he said. 'It's very flattering.'

In a way, it was. Jan collected her copy whilst shopping in the village. 'Bover Boy Bob!' the main headline screamed over a photograph of me and under the title 'Labour is Putting the Punch into Politics'. One of the 'party's Front Bench law and order spokesman', it said, 'has decided to put his knuckles where his mouth is. Step forward . . .'

As Peter Fisher volunteered in his cheerful and excited manner when he rang at lunchtime, it wouldn't do me any harm in the constituency – far from it. It would probably do me a great deal of good, especially if the reaction that Jan and I had experienced on Friday in Kirkby and in Stockbridge Village was any guide. The *Sun*, widely circulated amongst my constituents and voters, would also stiffen the support behind me.

The reaction to the live telephone interview with Jimmy Young on his morning radio programme confirmed all this. It was a relatively long interview. It was also the most difficult that I've had with Jimmy Young, and I must have done a dozen or more in the last few years. I sat on the sofa in the drawing room looking out of the French windows at my doves waiting on the lawn to be fed and repeated that I was confronted by a conspiracy conceived in Liverpool by Militant to take over my constituency, that they used the tactics of the caucus, of packing meetings and of intimidation, and that I could not give as much time and energy to my shadow ministerial duties as they needed or as I wanted to give.

Irritatingly, Jimmy Young said to me, 'You haven't solved the unemployment problem, though, have you, Robert, least that's what they say?'

'No,' I said, seeing in my mind's eye all the listeners shaking their heads and muttering 'oh well'. 'Nor has the Militant MP, Terry Fields. Nor has Eric Heffer. Nor can he while we have the Tories in power.'

Perhaps it was the unfairness of the question that made me speak for even longer than I normally do, and that's usually a reasonably long time, or so I'm told. I never notice.

'Does Mr Kilroy-Silk ever draw breath?' a listener called in to ask later.

'No, not very often,' I heard Jimmy Young say as Jan called me into the sunlit kitchen to listen. 'And I don't think that Robert will mind me saying that.'

I didn't.

Immediately the programme ended I received a call from my mole in the T & G. He thought that it was good, but he had bad news. Apparently Peter Killeen asked Bobby Owens for the number of members in the branches of the union that are affiliated to my constituency. As the number of delegates is based on the number of members in the branch living in the constituency it is obviously important to have this information if we are to confirm that the union's branches are entitled to the number of delegates that they have. The information was refused, and it was, my informant said, a very hostile meeting. 'At least,' he went on, 'Killeen will now know the score.' Apparently they have agreed to meet again on the 15th November to discuss the matter.

'Can you get me the membership figures?' I asked, hopefully.

'It's already being done. It may take some time but I'll make sure that you'll get them.'

I was glad to hear him say that, but I have to confess I'm not really all that worried. When I put the phone down this morning before telling Jan the bad news I was surprised by my lack of anxiety, and I still am. But the fact is it doesn't matter any more. I know now that whatever happens I shall survive. More than that, I know I'm in the right. It's good to be on the side of the good guys; it's also refreshing, indeed liberating, to be able to tell the truth.

What is interesting about the T & G and the Liverpool Militants is how brazen they've become. They're more confident and cocky. It's as if they feel that they're on the brink of taking over the party, or have already taken it over and know that they cannot be dislodged. Indeed, that is what many people on Merseyside are now saying. They allege that Militant has infiltrated the council and the Labour party so thoroughly that it will never lose effective control of either. In any event, Hatton is so cocksure that he not only attended a Militant rally in the Albert Hall last night, where he received 'an ecstatic reception' from 4000 Militant supporters, but he went on to attack Neil and suggested that he started 'to lead and represent your people in the same way that Thatcher leads and represents hers'.

It's turning out just as I thought – everybody will be to blame for what happens in Liverpool except Hatton and the Militants.

Tuesday 5th November 1985

What follows is going to sound a little like the Granada TV programme *What the Papers Say*, but I think it's important to provide a summary of today's press treatment of my resignation from the Front Bench for two reasons.

The first is that it demonstrates, with myself as the unfortunate example, how obsessed we politicians are with the media. Though we pretend otherwise to outsiders, we all know that much of what we say and do is with the intention of seeing ourselves in the newspapers or on television, especially on television. Of course, some MPs are more obsessed than others, and more blatant in their methods, but to some degree we have all fallen prey to the media. Indeed, we compliment each other, irrespective of party, not on having achieved or said anything of substance but on obtaining a lot of 'coverage'.

Perhaps the extreme example of this is the exchange that is said to have taken place between Cecil Parkinson, at the height of his trouble with Sara Keays, and David Penhaligon, the liberal MP for Truro, who, though a decent man, is not exactly famous for his tact or his sensitivity.

'Aye, aye,' Penhaligon is reputed to have said, as they approached each other from opposite ends of the long library corridor. 'Haven't you been doing well?' Cecil turned and strode away.

The same comment has been made to me several times today, even though the House is almost deserted.

The second excuse for including the press headlines is to give a flavour both of the interest in my difficulties and the different ways they are treated. I must confess, though, that I didn't expect to get a press like this, especially not the banner headlines. Among the surprises were the page two lead in *The Times* headlined 'Militant Move to Unseat Kilroy-Silk forces him to resign Commons Post', the top of the page *Daily Telegraph* 'Kilroy-Silk Quits Law and Order Role', and the *Guardian*'s 'Kilroy-Silk Stands Down to Fight Left-Wing Takeover'. The *Sun*'s 'Bovver Bob Quits Top Job over Left' was probably more to be expected, as was the *Daily Express*'s 'Forced Out Labour Moderate Quits Top Job to Fight Left'.

I began to realise just how interesting I was, for the moment, to the media. I'm 'hot property', according to Alan Coren. The phone hasn't stopped ringing all day. And the irony is, of course, that none of this was supposed to happen. My resignation was to have been overshadowed by the announcement of the Front Bench appointments following the annual elections to the Shadow Cabinet and Neil's reallocation of responsibilities. Instead, it dominated them.

Just before lunch I recorded an interview in the BBC studio in the Norman Shaw Building at Westminster with Sir Robin Day for the lunchtime BBC Radio 4 programme, *The World at One*. He was on top form. He surprised me with a couple of questions that I had not anticipated and forced me into saying things that I did not want to say. Perhaps it was because I hadn't thought much about the interview beforehand, and especially about what Neil said on the radio last night about not embarking on a purge of the Militants, but dealing with them by the normal democratic procedures of the party.

I should have heeded Jan's warning. As I left home this morning she reminded me to read the account of what Neil had said. Instead, I was too busy on the phone dealing with constituency problems. I thought that I'd done badly, been hustled. In fact when I heard the tape of it that Dominic recorded it wasn't at all bad. At least he and Jan said it was okay, and since they're both forthright critics that means it must be all right. In the course of the interview I said that I thought the Militants should be expelled from the party, but by the proper democratic procedures; that I would certainly like to see them expelled from my own constituency party; that, as my own party had not been properly managed, it ought to be disbanded; and that I would 'consider' standing as an Independent Labour candidate if deselected in favour of a Militant.

He asked me whether I thought the NEC should condemn Mr Mulhearn's candidature if he were to be selected instead of me. That, I said, would be a matter for the NEC. I refused to speculate about what it would do.

Then he changed tack.

'Would you expect Mr Kinnock to condemn it?'

'I can't say what Neil would do,' I replied. I stroked my thumb down the side of the glass of water that was on the table in front of me.

'Would you hope that he would condemn it?'

'I think he has to make his own decisions.'

'What would you hope that decision would be?'

'I hope that he would tell the truth.'

'What would telling the truth be, in so far as Mr Mulhearn is concerned?'

'Well, clearly – and you're doing a very good job of pushing me into a corner, aren't you, Robin? – clearly, the truth would be that Mr Mulhearn's membership of Militant Tendency makes him inappropriate for membership of the Labour party and inappropriate as a Labour candidate and potential Labour MP. Of course it does. There can be no doubt about that.'

So there we are. That felt better. I'd only had problems with the interview because I did not want him to be able to open up a conflict between me and Neil and because I did not want to embarrass Neil or get in the way of any overall strategy that he might have for dealing with the Militants. Still, I have to admit, it would be a lot easier if I could just speak for myself, speak my own mind.

At least I did that at the noisy and hilarious lunch immediately afterwards with Mike Hardwick, the managing director, and Don Atyeo, the editor of *Time Out*, at Magno's in Long Acre in Covent Garden. They want me to write a regular column for them. I'd discussed it with Mike and the former editor, Jerome Burne, in the summer when I wrote a couple of 'Second Opinion' pieces for them, one on acid rain and the other on the unit for mentally disturbed women in Holloway Prison that I wanted to see closed. Now they are ready to implement the idea. We discussed several ways of doing it and the different forms a political column could take.

'You know what I'd really like to do?' I said. 'I'd like to do a diary.'

That's what we agreed. Don asked me to do a couple of trial runs.

'No,' I said. 'No dress rehearsal. I'm doing it or I'm not.'

He agreed. He also agreed the fee. The copy has to be with them by noon on Monday.

I left feeling pleased but a little uncertain as to what I'm going to write about in such a relatively short period of time, especially as we are not in session and the State Opening of the new session of Parliament is not until tomorrow. There won't be anything exciting to report or any political gossip to regale the readers with until next week at the earliest. No matter, I'll find something.

The reason I want to do a diary is because of the experience of writing this. All right, so it's often a bore, especially when I have to write about the shenanigans in the constituency. But in the main I've enjoyed it. Perhaps it's been a therapy.

The news from the front line today could be interpreted as both promising and ominous. The good news from the GMBATU is that they do not have five delegates to my management committee from the Liverpool Militant-dominated Branch 5 as the list of delegates given to Peter Killeen by the constituency secretary claims. They only have three. They've already said Lawler is not a delegate, so that means another one off, but we don't yet know who.

There are now 139 delegates; I need 70 votes to win and I still have 66 and ten possibles. Are we getting there, albeit slowly?

The bad news, this time from the T & G, is that Peter Killeen was prevented from entering Transport House in Liverpool to verify the fact that Phil McSorley was indeed nominated as a delegate. He was going to meet the secretary of Phil McSorley's branch, 6/657, in order to be shown the correspondence book containing the copy of the letter nominating Phil to my management committee. Incredibly, he was met in the car park by Len McCluskey, the full-time political liaison officer who I have heard is no friend of mine, to put it at its best, and told that he had instructions from the regional secretary not to admit him.

I laughed. It's absolutely unheard of. What are they hiding? Why are they so desperate?

Jan was equally amazed when I met her this evening to go to dinner at the Press Club. It was the crime writer's annual dinner and, as for the past couple of years, we went as the guests of *Police Review* and its editor, Doreen May. She and David Plead, one of the assistant editors, were good company as usual.

Jan and I met at the House where I'd spent the afternoon dealing with my constituency correspondence and drove to Shoe Lane, so we didn't have enough time to go over all the events of the day. Most had to be left until the drive home down the M4 after dinner. It was a good day, but a long one.

Wednesday 6th and Thursday 7th November 1985

A major row is developing between the North West regional office of the Labour party and the regional office of the T & G over the union delegation to my management committee. Ernie Collett, the Labour party regional organiser for the North West, has written to Bobby Owens complaining about the way in which his assistant regional organiser, Peter Killeen, was prevented by Len McCluskey from meeting the branch secretary to verify that my supporter, Phil McSorley, was indeed a delegate. In his letter to the union Ernie says that he was 'shocked and dismayed' by Peter Killeen's report that he had been prevented from carrying out his errand. He goes on to say that he 'object(s) to this obstruction which is preventing us from doing our duty to the movement' and calls on Bobby Owen to 'rescind' his instructions and to supply them 'with the evidence necessary to ensure Phil McSorley's delegation to Knowsley North Constituency Labour Party'.

I find all this difficult to believe. I hadn't expected the Union to behave like this, even though I had been warned that it was more than likely that it would. But surely they must know that they will not be allowed to get away with all this, and that it will eventually become public.

There's no doubt that I've got enormous support from ordinary party members. I've had a tremendous number of letters in the last few weeks, every one of which offers encouragement and many of which promise help in canvassing if I need it. Most of the early letters seem to have been a result of Michael Cockerell's programme; dozens more arrived in response to the radio and newspaper coverage of my resignation from the Front Bench.

According to the *Guardian*, Frank Field is still collecting the names of MPs who will support me in the by-election that Frank is planning for me. Repeating an old story first published in the Liverpool *Daily Post*, it says that he aims to get fifty MPs 'who will be prepared to campaign for Bob in any by-election'. I must speak to Frank about this. I'm not going to be hustled into holding a by-election. I might lose. Nor do I want my colleagues putting themselves on the line for me. I really don't.

The Times also continues to report my story, as does the *Sun* with its 'Bob's in a Scrap' headline. *The Times* prefers the more informative 'Kilroy-Silk wants group disbanded', above an account of what I said to Robin Day on the radio on Tuesday. There was even a mention in a *Daily Express* editorial. I read them all while being driven in a BBC car to appear live on the early morning *Today* radio programme for a debate with John Cartwright of the SDP and Robert Jackson of the Tories on what we hoped to see in the Queen's Speech.

For some reason there was a massive snarl-up on the M40, so I walked into the studio and sat down just as Brian Redhead began asking the first question. He and John Timpson sat alongside each other at one end of the large circular table, perched on the edge of their seats and peering over their spectacles like a pair of wise old owls. Robert Jackson looked as if he'd been up all night. I'm sure he was wearing his pyjamas. The copious notes about the government's record that he had spread across the table in front of him suggested that he might have been. I only just resisted the temptation to say that he obviously couldn't even remember what his government had been doing for the last six years and needed the crutch of his notes and a heavily marked Central Office handout to remind him.

But then the Tories don't have to worry. No-one's interested in them. They're all interested in the battle within the Labour party, of which, unfortunately, I've now become something of a focus. And Liverpool. Liverpool rumbles on, with stewards from the GMBA-TU rejecting the report of the local authority treasurers, which has come to be called the Stonefrost Report, and its recommendations for rescuing Liverpool City Council.

I'd expected that the letter that I wrote to *The Times* about Kerr would have been published by now. It's strange that it hasn't appeared. They're usually scrupulous about corrections, especially on a matter like this.

Friday 8th November 1985

I wonder what's going on. *The Times* has a story by its 'political correspondent', which actually means Tony Bevins, quoting Neil as saying that he would make no intervention to 'help Mr Robert Kilroy-Silk, the embattled MP for Knowsley North, in his campaign against a Militant takeover of his constituency party. Asked what he would do if Mr Kilroy-Silk was deselected through Militant pressure, forcing a by-election, Mr Kinnock repeated: "He is well capable of looking after himself".'

The *Guardian*, on the other hand, has a story by its chief political correspondent under a headline 'Kinnock attacks Militant attempt to oust MP', which says that he 'gave strong backing' to me. It even goes on to say that his support of me 'would be welcomed by Labour MPs concerned at the effect of the Knowsley North row on the party's image in a region which includes some key target seats'.

Which is correct? I believe Bevins. I'm on my own. But then I always knew that I would be, and I think it's better like that. I can make my own decisions and fight the battle my way, and I've only got myself to blame for whatever happens. I won't owe anyone anything, either.

At least Mick Kelly, a party member in Knowsley and now a mature student on a trade union scholarship at Ruskin College, Oxford, has said that he is prepared to tell the story of how Jim McGinley tried to recruit him into the T & G. Mick's was one of the cases that I cited to Michael Cockerell, but unfortunately, he did not want to be publicly identified at the time and so he wasn't used in the film. That was a pity; it would have been fairly convincing proof of the conspiracy by the Militant. I've now received a letter from Mick confirming what he told me in August and saying that he was putting it.in writing in case it is ever of any use to me. Essentially, he says that the Militant supporter chairman of the constituency party approached him, even though he knew that he was a member of UCATT, and said that if Mick promised to vote for Tony Mulhearn he would get him membership of the T & G unemployed branch and a place on the management committee.

The same new-found determination to fight back was evident in the constituency today. It was displayed by many of those on the shop floor at the Myson's factory in Kirkby that I visited together with the Mayor, Frances Kneale. Virtually every person I spoke to insisted that I shouldn't let the Militants win and wished me luck. There was a good atmosphere. More than that, they weren't afraid of being seen with me on television. It was a big change from the reception I experienced some weeks ago when I wanted to visit the BICC plant in Prescot.

The Myson's factory visit was arranged weeks ago. Then, a few days ago, Michael Macmillan of ITN asked if they could film me in the constituency for a *News at Ten* item. He'd rung the managing director of Myson's, Clive Woods, who had been extremely helpful and co-operative. So the film crew and the reporter trailed around behind us all taking miles of film, out of which they will use a second or two. Unfortunately, every person who had the camera pointed at them expects to be on TV tonight.

They interviewed me separately outside the factory afterwards, as the office staff peered out of the windows. A lorry passed by. The driver thrust his arm out of the window and put his thumb up. They asked the same old questions, though. In effect these amounted to: 'Why don't people like you?' and 'What's wrong with you?' Of course, they're not put so crudely, but that's what it comes to. Once again I had to answer the charges of not living in the constituency and of having failed to bring full-time employment to Knowsley.

When they followed me to the Municipal Building in Kirkby, where I had some constituency business to deal with, and then to the town centre, at least they could see, as Michael Macmillan acknowledged, that I was neither unknown nor disliked by my constituents. He said he was amazed at the degree to which they know what the issue is. It reminded him of how it was in Northern Ireland. Not one person passed without a nod of acknowledgement or a hello. There were dozens of 'best of luck' handshakes. The trouble was they didn't get it all on film.

Saturday 9th November 1985

Bevins thinks that my first piece for *Time Out* is fine. That's a relief. I was worried about it. It's a new departure for me and I wasn't quite sure that what I had written worked. Jan said it did, and to have Tony's confirmation meant that it was definitely all right. Indeed, he laughed aloud at least twice when reading it in his high drawing room overlooking Widbrook Common at Cookham.

We called in to see them, as we often do at weekends on our way back from walking the dog along the Thames. This time there was no dog, hence no walk. We'd also only intended to stay for a short time, anxious to get back to the garden before dark, but Mishtu made tea, and more tea, and more tea. We stretched our legs in front of the fire, eased ourselves further into their large comfortable armchairs and quietly forgot the call of the cold, wet outdoors.

When we did return, and I rushed indoors just in time for the sporting programme's headlines, there was good news. We won away at Coventry and Manchester United lost away to Sheffield Wednesday, which means we're now only seven points behind. That won't be difficult to cover. I don't like the way Chelsea and Sheffield Wednesday are creeping up the table, however. Nor, for that matter, are Everton all that far away. It could be a close finish this year.

Then we had a disaster. Jan, distressed and anxious, rushed in with a soaking wet, bedraggled and shivering duck under her arm. Spats – so named because of her yellow and black feet – was one of our first ducks. She was part of a mixed brood and had been hatched and looked after by a Rhode Island Red hen. Jan bought the lot – what else? – just as she did with the cats. As the ducks were a present for me, and were like ducklings straight off an Easter card, she was forgiven.

Now it didn't look as if Spats would survive. There seemed to be no life left in her, but Jan was determined not to give up. She had fished Spats out of the water where for some unknown reason she had got stuck and had become exhausted and waterlogged. Jan blamed the Khaki Campbell for trying to mate with her. We've already lost a couple of ducks, drowned as a result of the drake's ardour. First we wrapped her in a large warm bath towel and gently patted her body. Then we placed her, still wrapped in the towel, near the coal fire in the drawing room. We collected an old single bar electric fire from the cellar and placed it behind her.

It didn't seem to be working. Normally one of the most aggressive and greedy of the ducks, she refused all water, bread and corn. Then Jan had a brain-wave – or at least I thought it was, though in retrospect it was obvious. She fetched a hair dryer. So instead of going to the theatre in London to see *Guys and Dolls*, as we were supposed to, we spent the rest of the evening slowly drying out each sorry-looking feather. And it worked: before our bedtime Spats was her usual raucous self, waddling around the room as if there had never been a problem.

Sunday 10th November 1985

When Sean Hughes told me that there was 'a groundswell of support' for me in the parliamentary party, I was surprised and flattered. I didn't expect it, and I still don't believe it. In any case, will the 'support' be there when I need it? I doubt it. I shall certainly not make any decisions on the assumption that it will be.

We were standing together in an icy wind in front of the war memorial outside the St Mary the Virgin church in Prescot waiting for the start of the annual remembrance service with the Mayor, Frances Kneale, and several hundred others. Though the sun shone from a clear blue sky it was very cold. The heavy fall of snow during the night had now cleared, but not in Wales. The Welsh hills were still a vivid white when we glimpsed them through the small windows of the seemingly rickety British Midland Fokker that brought us from Heathrow to Liverpool early this morning.

Sean was still whispering. 'Frank Field's got a list of over 70 members who'd be willing to come and help in the by-election,' he said. He looked round carefully to make sure that no-one could hear. 'They can't take the whip away from all of us,' he added, confidently.

Christ. I don't want a by-election. I've already been elected, with a majority of 17,000. I've been returned for the lifetime of this parliament and it has a few more years to run yet. The difficulty now is that I can't say that I don't want a by-election without it looking as if I've backed down.

We laid our wreaths at the foot of the war memorial and stood in silence. This is always an emotional day for me – always has been for my family. Apart from the fact that my own father and his younger brother, Robert, were killed in the war, my father's best friend and later my stepfather died, as I've said, just a few days after I was elected, at the early age of 53. Jan's father died at an even earlier age.

A single seagull drifted across the sky as the siren in the nearby BICC factory sounded the end of the two minutes' silence and the colour party from the Huyton Air Training Corps raised their standards. Jan hugged me as if she were cold, but, as we both knew, for comfort, as we strode into the dark church for the service.

'You'll win easy. You know that, don't you?' Sean said from behind as he joined his wife, Tricia. 'No problem.' He seems to be excited by the prospect of a battle virtually on his own doorstep. It's well known that he has no love for the Militants, either in Liverpool or Knowsley.

He and many others had seen the story in the *Mail on Sunday*, inspired by Peter Fisher and entitled 'I was asked to rig vote', which gave an account of Mick Kelly's accusations about Jim McGinley.

'Jimmy McGinley phoned,' Mick Kelly was reported as saying, 'and said that if I would give a firm commitment to vote for Tony Mulhearn he would fix me up with credentials via the transport union as an unemployed member.' McGinley said the 'allegations are outrageous'. But then he would, wouldn't he?

No-one, however, mentions Woodrow Wyatt's brief endorsement in his column in the *News of the World*, where he refers to me as the 'reasonable' Labour MP, although several people among the party that we had coffee with afterwards in Prescot Civic Hall mentioned the *Sunday Times* story claiming that regional officials of the Labour party are being obstructed in their attempts to verify the credentials of the delegates from the T & G by officials of the union.

It's all beginning to boil very nicely. We shall add more to the pot when necessary.

Monday 11th November 1985

I saw Neil this morning, at my request. I was in fact fulfilling a promise that I had made to a freelance Merseyside journalist to tell Neil what he had been told by John Hamilton, the leader of Liverpool City Council, about his intention towards the Militants. It all seemed melodramatic. Nevertheless, I faithfully reported what had been said to me and Neil was not surprised. In spite of all the difficulties he was having with the Militants he looked relaxed and showed no hint of the strain that I felt was on my own face. Then we talked about me.

I could see the red London buses travelling towards Waterloo Bridge from the lead-lined windows of his room underneath Big Ben.

He thought that I should 'tone down' my campaign. It was clear that the by-election threat was worrying him, and he was obviously relieved when I told him that there would not be one. I wonder if I have done the right thing? Probably not. Neil will do what he can to help me, I know that, but he might have had a little extra incentive if he wanted to avoid a by-election. I've now removed that threat. Never mind.

He didn't mention it, but the four-column spread in today's *Guardian* headlined 'Party Officials may bar Union Delegates over Kilroy-Silk Clash with Militant' must have upset him. It was a reasonably thorough, though incomplete, account of the way in which the regional Labour party officials are struggling with officers of the T & G to reduce its delegation to the correct number; how the reselection might have to be delayed; how a by-election was in prospect; how I had resigned as a shadow minister; how I had called for the disbanding of the party; and, perhaps most worrying to Neil, how I had received 'tacit support' from the Labour leader. There was also an amazing letter attacking me, written by four of my parliamentary colleagues, comrades and friends. It said that my threat to force a by-election, and Frank Field's efforts to enlist the support of MPs to campaign for me, was an interference in the democratic procedure of the Labour party.

That is, of course, a very serious crime – yet it did not deter them from rushing to commit it themselves, by telling my party what to do. It seems as if they couldn't wait to point out that any MPs whom Frank might recruit would lay themselves open to expulsion from the party, as indeed they would. Standing against an official Labour candidate, or supporting anyone who does so, means expulsion from the party. The letter made me angry, because it was a clear invitation to my party to vote for Tony Mulhearn. It didn't surprise me that Terry Fields should be the leading signatory. He's one of them. Indeed, without his Militant label and supporters he's what Liverpudlians call a 'no-mark', of no account. But why should Eddie Loyden, Bob Wareing and, above all, Allan Roberts, the MP for Bootle, lend their names to this tirade? There was no need for it. It seems, on reading it again, to be a gratuitous attack on me by people who affect friendship. I must speak to them. I can't wait, in fact. Their reasons, especially those of Wareing and Roberts, will be interesting to hear.

I talked at length to two experienced members of the NEC today. On the evidence about my party that they already possessed, and which I supplemented, they advised me that there is an overwhelming case for an inquiry into the party with a view to it being disbanded. They suggest that I take steps to trigger the process now, but I'm not sure. I want to continue collecting evidence that will invalidate the delegates who should not be on my management committee, and I'm keen to hold the reselection in a month's time as planned. But is my reluctance to heed their advice based on the belief that I can win on 10th December, or on my distaste for the whole thing and a desire not to prolong it? I think it is a little of both.

I was also annoyed with *The Times*. They say they did not receive the letter about Kerr that I delivered by hand. I only rang them to enquire when it would be published because Peter Fisher told me that they had also refused to print a letter from two ex-Labour MPs who are on my management committee, Walter Aldritt and Frank Marsden.

The letter was signed by these two ex-MPs and JPs, and two district councillors, Peter Fisher and Michael Murphy. Peter quoted it to me on the phone: 'What Mr Kerr forgot to mention was that he is at the forefront of the attack on Robert Kilroy-Silk, and while he may nominally be the press officer, he doesn't speak on our behalf . . .' The letter goes on, he said, to confirm that the delegates are asked to 'step outside', that elderly women delegates 'are barracked', and that I was an 'outstanding MP' and had every right to go on the offensive. I made sure that he would send me a copy.

The Times letters editor had no explanation of why a letter from such eminently respectable and obviously experienced people on such an important matter was not published. 'We can't publish them all,' he said.

At least *Country Living* is intending to publish an article I wrote on herons in its March issue next year. Yes, that's right, herons. A couple of months ago Jan and I saw one, our first, perched on a notice board in the middle of the Thames near the weir at Boulters Lock, Maidenhead. Being curious I looked up some information about them when I got home and discovered that the Ministry of Agriculture and Fisheries issues licences for them to be shot if they are thought to be damaging commercial fish stocks. Phil Drabble, the naturalist, has written that this is nonsense, and he confirmed as much to me on the telephone. According to him, the herons that live near his home in Staffordshire consume perch and eels, both of which prey on trout. Even in the unlikely event of certain herons living exclusively on a diet of trout, their daily intake of between 330 and 500 grams is a small loss. I therefore put down some parliamentary questions on the subject to the Ministry of Agriculture, and to the Secretary of State for Scotland, asking how many licences they have issued and how many herons have been destroyed.

The answers showed that in England two herons were shot in 1983, four in 1984 and that licences for the killing of six birds have been issued so far this year. In Scotland, however, 34 herons were killed legally in 1983, and 44 in 1984. I was upset by this destruction of the shy and graceful bird that we had seen waiting patiently for its supper, especially as it is being done for commercial reasons and on behalf of commercial undertakings that are not prepared to be publicly identified. So I wrote an article on the subject and *Country Living* have now accepted it for publication.

I shall be criticised when it appears, of course. I am supposed neither to be interested in such things nor to have the time to write about them, still less to enjoy it. Sod it. I am what I am.

Tuesday 12th November 1985

Things must be getting really bad. Denis Healey stopped me at the Members' entrance tonight. 'Hello, Bob,' he said warmly. Then, arm outstretched, he shook my hand firmly and with feeling. 'All the best.' I felt as if I was about to be sent over the top at Anzio, never to return. Perhaps I am.

Clement Freud added to my sense of unease. He sidled up to me as I was speaking to Joe Ashton while waiting to vote in the Aye lobby at ten o'clock on our amendment to the Queen's Speech, which sets out the legislative programme for this Parliament.

'Would it damage you very much if I came to speak for you at your by-election?' he asked, mischievously.

'Aye, it would,' Joe answered for me. 'Stay out. You're not needed. He's got enough of us.'

'All right then.' Clement retreated, thankfully. 'I'll tell you a joke instead.' It wasn't very good, but then his rarely are. Joe Ashton's version was much better. And cruder.

I suspect that what occasioned all this, and the smirks from some of my colleagues, was the story in today's *Times*. I hadn't seen it. I didn't see it until we got home well after midnight.

I left home at six-thirty this morning in order to get to Bournemouth for ten o'clock to speak at the Conference of Prison Chaplains on *Penal Reform: A Strategy for the Future*. I spoke for fifty minutes, without notes, answered questions for ninety minutes and left the room, amazingly, to a standing ovation. I hope it wasn't in sympathy.

I arrived at the House in time to deal with the more pressing phone messages and sign the letters left for me by Sarah. I had a quick word with Noni about the work she is doing on police clear-up rates, before dashing off to speak at Arthur Andersen's in Surrey Street on the political implications of the Data Protection Act, on which I had been the Opposition spokesman during its passage through Parliament. It was only when Jan collected me from there at six o'clock to take us both to a reception at Winfield House, the American Ambassador's beautiful home in Regents Park, that I learned about *The Times* story.

'What do you think?' Jan asked breathlessly, almost as soon as I got into the car. She looked lovely.

'You look great.'

'Not that,' she smiled as I kissed her on the cheek. 'About *The Times*.'

'It's all right,' I answered. I was worried about the way that she was weaving the car through the rush-hour traffic along the Aldwych.

'All right!' she exclaimed. 'Neil attacks you and it's all right?'

My edition of *The Times*, which I bought when I changed trains at Reading en route for Bournemouth, had a page two story about the Prescot East Branch's decision to move a resolution calling for the expulsion of the constituency chairman Jim McGinley on the grounds that he was a supporter of Militant. Jan's *Times*, a later edition, did not have that story. Instead, in the same place in the newspaper, it had a large headline that announced, 'Kinnock Critical of Kilroy-Silk tactics'. It reported that Neil would be writing to me, at the instigation of Eric Heffer, to 'advise me to tone down my campaign'.

I couldn't believe it. I couldn't believe that Neil would agree to such a thing, not when proposed by Eric Heffer of all people. I was livid. It was a good job, after all, that Jan was driving.

'What's it got to do with Heffer?' she asked.

'I suppose someone in Liverpool has had a word with him.'

'What will you say?'

'Get stuffed.'

I couldn't wait. I don't know why but I thought about my father and his unknown grave. Jan and I have been several times to the little graveyard up the hill above Dinard in France where some of his comrades are buried and where there is a grave, perhaps his, of a 'sailor from *Charybdis*'.

He died, we're told, to protect democracy. Well, perhaps he did. Whatever: there's no way that I'm going to allow myself to be silenced by the Militants and the likes of the Heffers of this world.

It made me think of the inscription that we both saw yesterday on one of the small wooden crosses outside Westminster Abbey for those who had been killed in the Falklands. We walked in the damp and the early evening gloom to pay our respects and to admire the wreaths and the crosses laid out in rows on the glistening grass. All the crosses for the Falklands had names on them. Many also had inscriptions. One, in a biro scrawl that was beginning to blur from the rain, had something about the responsibility of the living to protect the gift of freedom given to us by the dead. Yes, it's a cliché. No matter, it affected me deeply. Perhaps that was because I feel a responsibility for those deaths and injuries in those far away islands. I do. I wanted that Task Force sent and I've supported the operation ever since. But I felt ill and could not sleep for its entire duration.

Of course, the best answer to the Militants and to the sour and embittered Heffer is not to quote that inscription but to win. And winning, as I was repeatedly told during the brief reception in the rooms that Walter Annenburg had 'refurbished' at Winfield House, is what I have to do. Not for myself: I'm just the figurehead. I've got to win, they insist, for the Labour party, for democracy. 'For the sake of the country,' one Tory said. It was heady stuff. I didn't really believe it all; though to be fair there was no doubting their sincerity.

Andrew Faulds, the actor MP for Warley East, was one of the most vigorous and outspoken. In fact, he barged across the room and burst into our group when he saw me.

'Look here, Kilroy,' he began. 'I've never liked you and you've never liked me but you mustn't let these bastards win. You've got to fight them. You mustn't give in.' He added with emphasis, 'Don't let anyone put you off.'

It was a message that was repeated by Terry Davis, my mother's MP in Birmingham, Hodge Hill, and his wife and former NEC member, Anne, Kevin McNamara, the member for Kingston upon Hull North, and many, many more. But I wonder whether they will be there if it comes to the crunch.

We thought that we'd get away from all this at Ruth's relaxed and beautifully decorated new house, where we went on for dinner, a dinner that I had to interrupt to go back to the House for the vote at ten. Not a chance. Everyone wanted to talk about it. They all seemed fascinated by the political goings-on, particularly Nick Fraser who has just returned from Liverpool after filming for Channel 4. Like Bevins and everyone else who has experienced the politics of Liverpool, he was appalled by it all, and especially the atmosphere of intimidation that prevails.

Wednesday 13th November 1985

I spoke to Allan Roberts today.

'Why did you sign the Militants' letter, Allan?'

'Well . . . er . . . um.' Anne Page, a committee clerk for the PLP whom he had been speaking to, moved away. John Evans, whom I was with, waited alongside. We were in the Members' Lobby.

'Why did you?'

He gathered confidence from my aggression.

'Because I believed it.'

'Because you believe it?'

'Yes.' But he didn't say it with conviction.

'What do you believe, Allan?'

'That parties should be able to choose their own candidates.'

'I see,' I said sarcastically. 'And you felt that so strongly that you had to write to the *Guardian* about it. Do you write letters to newspapers attacking your colleague – someone you call a friend – every time you believe something, Allan? Why haven't you written in to attack Hatton and the Militants whom you're always criticising privately? Why haven't you written about them?'

This continued for a while.

He then said. 'I've already had the Militants in Bootle moving a resolution asking me to explain myself for my public statements on Liverpool.'

Would you believe it? A comrade, a colleague, a friend – who didn't even have the decency to tell me that he'd written the letter, let alone warn me in advance.

As for Bob Wareing, he was all simpering and incoherent when I asked him his reasons in the Tea Room yesterday. But he insisted that he believed in what he was doing.

It also seems that the T & G intend to brazen it out and to try and compel Peter Killeen and the Labour party to accept their delegates. According to my friend in the T & G, Peter Killeen is doing a good job and is being very tough. He's insisting that they abide by the rules and that everything must be seen to be in order. That's confirmed from what I've heard from the GMBATU. He's caused great consternation there by asking for the number of members of the Militant-dominated Liverpool Branch 5 that live in my constituency. In order to qualify even for their newly reduced number of three delegates they must have 201 members living in Knowsley North. They have no idea how many they have.

At least I now know the membership of the T & G branches affiliated to my constituency. I already have the figures and they don't add up – it's clear that many do not have enough members to support the delegates. Thus, the 6/556 branch – the Pendletons Ice Cream factory branch in Kirkby – has only 304 members overall but five delegates, which would require 401 members, all of them living in Knowsley North. Otis Elevators' Kirkby T & G branch 6/507 has 98 members and two delegates: even if all 98 members lived in Knowsley North it would only be entitled to one delegate. Best of all is branch 6/612, that of the regional secretary of the T & G, Bobby Owens. An unemployed branch, it has only 263 members – who cannot all live in my constituency, surely – but five delegates, for which it ought to have a membership of 401, at least. The other unemployed branch with five delegates, 6/538, does have sufficient members, just. It has 446. But it is extremely unlikely that 401 of them will be constituents of mine.

Similar considerations apply to several of the other branches. There is even better news, too. Some of the T & G branches have been sending delegates to other Merseyside constituencies on the same membership. I've asked those of my Merseyside Parliamentary colleagues that I can trust how many delegates they have from branches that are also affiliated to my constituency. I've also had my T & G friend burrowing for me, and we've come up with gold. Let's take just two examples: the two branches that each send five delegates – all Militant supporters or fellow travellers – to my constituency party management committee. First is T & G branch 6/612, the one that Bobby Owens is a member of. It has 263 members throughout Merseyside, which would entitle it to no more than three delegates in any one constituency, assuming that all the members lived there. In fact, it has 24 delegates that we have counted so far and we haven't covered all the constituencies. That means, in effect, that the branch is claiming a membership of more than 2,400. The same is true of T & G branch 6/522. It has an actual

135

membership of 638 but at least 24 delegates, equivalent to 2,400 plus members. I think we've got them.

I was told that the T & G regional official would be meeting the Labour party regional officials on 15th November to determine the delegation, and that the T & G would offer a reduction of no more than four delegates. He told me which these would be. They're no fools. They're all people whom Peter Fisher has already challenged as not having been members of the party for the required 12 months. We don't know if Peter is correct, because they control the membership lists, but it's a strange coincidence that the ones whom he believes to be ineligible anyway are the same ones that the union has apparently chosen to discard.

I mentioned some of this to Frank Field as we stood at the Bar of the Chamber of the House of Commons listening to John Biffen winding up the debate on the economy. As usual on these occasions we couldn't hear a word he was saying. No-one was listening anyway. The House was full but everyone was either talking or barracking. We were waiting, with everyone else, for the ten o'clock vote. Then we could go home. The rush out of the lobby doors, through the Members' Lobby, down the side marble stairs to the Members' Entrance, a quick plucking of a coat from the named coat hook, and the dash outdoors to get a taxi or hustle down the concrete stairs to the car park, is just like the nightly exodus from the factory where I worked for a couple of summers and in which my stepfather spent his life.

Frank has been to see Neil about the letter that Neil was reported to be sending him. Without waiting for it to be delivered Frank marched into Neil's office and asked what it was all about. Neil told him to stop pushing for a by-election.

Frank said he had refused.

'Well, that's it then,' Neil said. 'We'll lose the next election and the next one.'

'You'd better do something to stop it then, hadn't you?' Frank said. 'You'd better help Kilroy.'

'Thanks, Frank,' I said, not sure that he had done me any favour, though he was undoubtedly sincere.

'We can do without being hauled over the coals,' he said. 'If anything, what we need is a little political cuddling.'

He was right. I liked that expression. He's enjoying my predicament far more than he enjoyed his own and he was disappointed when I told him to do as Neil asked.

Thursday 14th November 1985

I phoned Ernie Collett, the Labour Party's regional organiser in the North West. I knew that he was to meet the T & G official tomorrow to try to sort out the mess of their delegation. I told him that they would only offer to remove four delegates. To be sure that he fully understood my determination about this, I told him to tell them that I would not be prepared to go ahead with the reselection until I was satisfied that the T & G had no more delegates than it had paid for and was entitled to under the party rules. If necessary, I said, I will use the law to back me up.

He got huffy. He misunderstood. Instead of realising that I was trying to strengthen his hand in dealing with them, he construed my remarks as a combination of threats and of telling him how to do his job. He's a nice man, Ernie, but I do wonder whether he can sort this out. He spoke to me of the wrong branches and the wrong delegates, which did not exactly inspire me with confidence. I had visions of him coming back waving a piece of paper saying they've backed down and reduced the delegates by a dozen and then find that they've got rid of all my supporters, like Peter Fisher.

Never mind, he did at least confirm that a very acrimonious correspondence has passed between him and Bobby Owens on the subject of the refusal of the union to allow party officials to check the books.

In the middle of all this, I dealt with the voluminous constituency correspondence on every conceivable subject that there seems to be nowadays, which Sarah handles so competently and professionally. Amazingly, since the Queen's speech was only a few days ago and the Bill has not yet been published, I've already had several letters opposing the proposal to allow shops to open on Sundays. I know I will get lots more letters on that particular subject. Many of the authors of the letters will no doubt be the same as those who write to oppose abortion and research on embryos. I shall never be able to placate them. Let's hope that one day they will write to me on a subject that I can enthusiastically endorse. There were also dozens of phone calls from troubled constituents, including one whose fiancé was about to be deported, which I managed to prevent. I managed to get into the Chamber for Question Time and Prime Minister's Questions, after which I escaped to my small white-walled room to write my fortnightly article for *Police Review*.

This time I took Law and Order as the subject. It will be the issue of this session of Parliament. What we have to ensure is that it remains our issue. With an increase in serious crime since this Government came into office of 40 per cent, with offences involving firearms up by 48 per cent, vandalism up 63 per cent and burglaries by 59 per cent, we have a good case to make and we must make it. My only regret is that I have neither the will, the enthusiasm or the commitment to make it while I'm so internally miserable and debilitated, though outwardly smiling.

I'm beginning to envy other people, something I've never done before. I envy the apparent absence of pressure, the lack of aggravation, the clear sign that they're not being harassed as I am. I felt this tonight when we had dinner in Holland Park at the home of Michael and Bridget Cockerell, together with journalists Emma Soames and James McManus and the novelist Piers Paul Reid and his wife Lucy. They seem to have such untroubled lives. I envy the fact that – unlike me – they can do as they please, be themselves, and not have to keep looking over their shoulder to see who is watching and hoping they'll make a mistake.

Friday 15th November 1985

We were right about the ASTMS delegates, or at least one of them. He's not a member of the party and does not even pay the trade union levy to the party. That's one more to be knocked off. It's a slow process, but at least it means there are now 138 delegates; I still need 70 of them and I still have 66 and ten possibles.

We're not there yet, but perhaps it won't be necessary. I told Geoff and Frances Kneale about the advice that I was getting to seek an enquiry into the running of the party with the intention of having it disbanded and reformed when I had dinner tonight at their home in Dunfold Close, Kirkby, before starting my surgeries. They were adamantly in favour of doing it. Indeed, the prospect of actually being able to get rid of the known Militants delighted and encouraged them. No wonder, since the Militants have not only taken over the constituency party but have also extended their tentacles into the council. One of the longest–serving and most respected of the councillors in Kirkby, Frank Lawler, was challenged and defeated by them last year. They've already got Peter Fisher in their sights, naturally, and others will follow. The problem with these other councillors is that they don't realise it yet or, more probably, still refuse to acknowledge the inevitable. They don't seem to understand that the Militants they are now appeasing and making compromises with, the apparently friendly faces they are consorting with, are already plotting their demise.

During a long day in the constituency I was repeatedly engaged in conversation – even in the streets – about my own battle with the Militants and the difficulties in Liverpool. The opinion is unanimous: they have to be kicked out of the Labour party. No-one said anything different to me.

The disturbing part of all this is that there was an element of criticism of Neil. They expect him to back up his strong words in Bournemouth with action in Liverpool. 'And what is this about him needing evidence that they're Militants?' several said in reference to Neil's expressed view that if anyone brought him evidence that party members were also members of Militant he would see that they were expelled. 'We all know who they are,' they insisted. 'Everybody does.' The positive reaction to Neil's Conference speech will be destroyed if he fails to follow it through. But I'm not really the one to tell him, am I?

In any case, we shouldn't have to be spending our time and energy fighting an enemy within. We should be campaigning against the Tory Government, capitalising on its mismanagement of the economy and its acceptance of horrendous levels of unemployment. This is certainly what the real battle should be all about on Merseyside, where, according to the Government's own figures given in answer to parliamentary questions from me this week, the rate of unemployment is 21.1 per cent. The same answer disclosed that there are over 20,000 unemployed in the relatively small borough of Knowsley.

These are the facts to which we should be drawing the attention of the public and to which we should be offering remedies, but instead we are bogged down in a vicious and distracting battle with a group of revolutionary Trotskyites. The only winners are the Tories and the SDP Liberal Alliance; the sure losers are our own people. But then they will never win if we don't hold on to the Labour party.

Saturday 16th November 1985

Of nine people at our dinner table tonight, only Jan was not of Irish Catholic descent. Terry and Helen Wogan, Alan and Anne Coren, Joyce Hopkirk, Bill Lear and Carmen Callil all are.

Carmen arrived very late. She'd got lost in the dark rainsoaked lanes of Buckinghamshire, and when she rang for directions from the Burnham Golf Club we put Helen Wogan on the phone as neither Jan or I knew where it was. Helen didn't last long.

'I think we'd better go and get her,' Helen said to me, her hand over the mouthpiece. 'She's likely to go back home if we don't. I'll go,' she offered.

Terry and I went in his Rolls instead. We could see Carmen at the bar as we drove into the car park.

'I didn't know that Labour MPs drove around the countryside in Rolls Royces,' she said, busily adjusting her hat and scarf as I collected her on the steps. 'Do you always do that?' she asked as she strode purposefully towards her car parked alongside Terry's.

'Hello,' she nodded curtly at his face beaming out of the driver's window. I think she thought he was the chauffeur. Then she stopped, looked again and said 'Oh, I know you. You're Terry Wogan. Hello,' and flinging her scarf over her shoulder she marched on.

She drove all the way to our house in third gear, but I didn't tell her.

It was a tremendous evening. How could it have been otherwise? Alan Coren is probably the most naturally witty and spontaneously funny man I know and Terry, of course, has hundreds of hilarious stories. Not even the lingering physical tiredness of the journey back from Knowsley earlier in the day or the fact that not one of them had seen my new column in *Time Out* spoilt it. It was a good end to an evening that had begun with the news of Liverpool's defeat of West Bromwich and Manchester United's draw with Tottenham, thus putting us still second but now only five points behind. We only need to win two games, and for Manchester to lose two, and we'll be back where we belong, on top.

140

Sunday 17th November 1985

We cleared the leaves in a biting wind, watched as always by our increasingly tame robin. I felt very depressed. The collecting and composting of the garden rubbish seemed to be pointless, for a reason that I cannot explain. It also meant that I had too much time to think. Whereas I would normally have been thinking of new plans for the garden and of how what I was preparing would look in the spring, I was preoccupied with the troubles in my constituency.

I've had enough of it all. I keep asking myself why I should let it dominate and spoil my life. Worse still, it is now intruding into the lives of the kids, who are constantly being asked about my problems by their friends, their friends' parents, their teachers or just people they meet. They say they don't mind, but I wonder.

And the phone never stops ringing. There's always someone who wants me to comment on the latest antics of the Liverpool Militants, the most recent pronouncement by Neil or someone else on the subject or, as happens almost every day now, who is just ringing to see if 'anything is happening'. That sort of thing is annoying and very disruptive. I even had Carol West of BBC Radio's *The World At One* asking if she could accompany me in Knowsley North as I fought for reselection. She obviously had a notion that it would be like a by-election and that I would be tramping the streets urging people to vote for me. She seemed disappointed when I told her that the 'selectorate' amounted to no more than 140, that their votes were already largely committed, and that all decisions would be made behind closed doors.

In spite of all this I managed to write my diary for *Time Out*, with considerable help from Jan and Natasha. I told the story of Denis Healey, or *Major* Denis Healey, as Jan suggested – a nice touch that – wishing me luck as if I was about to go over the top at Anzio; I said that I was still waiting for the letter from Neil instigated by Heffer and recounted the confrontation with Allan Roberts. We sat at the table in the kitchen drinking coffee in the early evening and argued about it. Jan and Natasha said there was too much of me in it. I said that's what you'd expect from a diary. They disagreed. They ganged up against me. I backed down in the end, because they're right.

I did, however, manage to finish Norman Mailer's *Tough Guys*

Don't Dance, which Jan gave me for Christmas – yes, it's taken that long to find the time. I'd forgotten how powerful a writer Mailer is. Why can't I write like he does? It's a crazy, bizarre story but which is totally believable and stunningly told. He obviously meets women like the blonde, pneumatic and voraciously sexy Jessica and Patty Lareine every day. I don't.

The book reminded me of William Boyd's *Stars and Bars*, also a Christmas present, from Dominic – or was it Natasha? I shall get into trouble if I don't get it right. That was almost as weird and as compelling, but not in the same class, I think, as his *An Ice Cream War*, which I read somewhere in the sun some years ago and which I would be proud to have authored.

That's what I should be doing, I said to myself: writing. Not because I presume to emulate those I've just read, but because it's what I enjoy. So I wrote this. And I wrote it as I always do: fast, by hand, without a thought beyond the first sentence and without re-reading or correction. I write as I think. I hope, when I re-read it all, that it's coherent.

Monday 18th November 1985

I deliberately refrained from ringing my contact in the T & G today to find out what happened at the meeting on Friday between the regional officials of the union and of the party, which was supposed finally to resolve the problems over the T & G delegation. I didn't want all the hassle that would be involved in thinking about what he would tell me, getting angry and depressed and having to make decisions about it. Was it cowardice or laziness? I don't know. Perhaps a bit of both. It's also become boring.

It was easier, more rewarding and certainly more satisfying, to deal with the numerous problems that my constituents brought to me at my surgeries on Friday. A morning on the phone and dictating letters for Sarah, and most of the afternoon likewise, provided some of the job satisfaction I needed.

However, I wasn't entirely happy with the parliamentary reply that I received today from the Arts Minister, Richard Luce, about the future of Prescot Museum when Merseyside County Council disappears next March. The museum is run jointly by the Knowsley and Merseyside Councils and concentrates on the history of the town, especially that part of it connected with the manufacture of watches and clocks, as well as mounting special displays and exhibitions.

I called in a few days ago to look at their latest exhibition on the American Red Indians. The local schools will all visit and use it as a focus for special projects. The staff were anxious about the prospects for themselves and the museum when responsibility for it is vested in the Merseyside Residuary Body, which will be taking on some of the functions of the County Council next April.

Unfortunately Richard Luce was unable to provide the reassurances that I was seeking. It will be for all the parties involved in responsibility for the museum in the future to discuss what is to happen, he said. That will be no help or consolation to the anxious staff, but they are not alone. The same anxieties and uncertainties are being experienced by thousands of hard-working people in voluntary and other organisations in London and the other metropolitan areas. It's a disgrace that they should be subjected to this upheaval and that services should be destroyed just because the Prime Minister took a dislike to Ken Livingstone.

Even more worrying is that the Paymaster General, Alan Clark, told me that another 7,000 redundancies are due to occur on Merseyside, 687 of which will be in Knowsley and 62 in my town of Kirkby. They will add to the ever-lengthening and increasingly hopeless dole queues. There are now over 23,000 people on Merseyside who have been unemployed for more than four years. Two and a half thousand of these are my constituents. I cannot describe the despair that many of them feel, and which many, especially the men in their middle fifties who are afraid that they will never work again, express to me in my surgeries. The fact that there are only 190 vacancies for the 20,000 people unemployed in Knowsley, as Alan Clark informed me in answer to another question, gives an indication of the scale of the problem. Then Norman Tebbitt has the cheek to tell them to get on their bikes and the Prime Minister has the effrontery to lecture me on my constituents' inability or refusal to set up their own businesses mending electric kettles.

Jan collected me from the Commons just after six o'clock so that we could go to the launch party of *Mirror* editor Mike Molloy's novel, *The Black Dwarf*, at the *Mirror* headquarters, before returning to the House to eat a rushed dinner in the cafeteria and to vote at ten o'clock. He has been talking about his book for months, just as I did about mine, no doubt, a couple of years ago.

I couldn't find a copy of the book, however. Robert Maxwell's daughter seemed to possess the only one. Joyce Hopkirk suggested facetiously that they were all locked away in a metal chest, but I couldn't find that either. Apart from being there as a friend, I was also, in my own eyes at least, present in my new role as a *Time Out* columnist. Indeed, all the gossip columnists were there: Nigel Dempster from the *Daily Mail,* Peter Tory of the *Star,* who I think is actually the best and most interesting of them all, Peter Hillmore of the *Observer,* Paul Callan of the *Mirror,* the William Hickey of the day from the *Express,* while the captivating Angela Gordon represented *The Times.* And what did they all do? They talked to each other, of course. No-one else could be as interesting or have such lurid stories. Only Peter Hillmore had noticed my *Time Out* column; he wouldn't help me with any stories for it though.

Jeffrey Archer, the former Tory MP for Louth and now vice-chairman of the Tory party and successful novelist, was also present. The last time I spoke to him was when Parliament was dissolved in 1974 and he announced that he was in danger of going bankrupt and would not be standing for re-election. We walked out across the cobblestones of the members' entrance while I commiserated with him.

'Oh, it's all right,' he said confidently. 'I shall go away and write a bestselling novel and make a million.'

Hmm, I thought, so will we all.

Joe Haines, who worked for Harold Wilson as his press secretary when he was at Number 10 and now advises Robert Maxwell at the *Mirror,* wanted to know about Knowsley. We've talked about it and the Militants before. He wants to help. He's a good man, Joe: he's one of the most experienced and sharpest of political operators and a superb journalist. He represents the 'real' Labour party and is angry at what is being done to it.

At the moment, the main damage, of course, is still being done by the Militants in Liverpool. The meeting between the national trade union leaders and the councillors in London not only broke up without an agreement but ended with Hatton insulting the new general secretary of the GMBATU, John Edmonds, and saying that he was out of touch with his members. Only Hatton, it seems, is in touch with anyone or anything.

144

Tuesday 19th November 1985

I received a copy of the list of delegates that the T & G submitted to the officials of the Labour party on Friday. It's a strange list.

It has been clear for a long time that whatever else the regional secretary of the T & G is doing he is not going out of his way to help me. Indeed, everything that the union does at a regional level seems designed to hinder my reselection. The list is an example. The union has paid £111 in affiliation fees to cover all its delegates. At £5 per delegate this would work out at 22 delegates, whereas in fact they have 36, so the union has been asked to reduce the number of delegates. It will choose who shall be removed. If fourteen Militant supporters were removed I would have no problem; the figures show that. There would then be 124 delegates, and to win I would have to get 63 votes. I've 66 definite promises and a further ten that might, probably will, vote for me. It's not a comfortable margin – but it's a winning one. So the T & G's attitude is crucial.

And what have they done? They've ordered the apportionment of their affiliation fees in such a way as to maximise the number of delegates they can have. Their reasoning goes like this. Leaving aside the number of members that a branch has, the union is required to pay an affiliation fee of 5p for every member, with a minimum of £5. Thus a £5 affiliation fee would represent 100 members and entitle the union to one delegate. An affiliation fee of £5.05p would, however, mean that it had affiliated on 101 members and so entitle it to two delegates. A £10 payment would also have the same result but a fee of £10.05p could be for 201 members and allow it to have three delegates. In effect, they can get an extra delegate for an extra 5p, and this is what they've done. In order to make the £111 go as far as possible and cover as many delegates as possible, they've said that the affiliation for some branches is £5.05p, entitling that branch to two delegates. They've done it for several branches. Thus the new 6/538 branch covering the Kirkby Unemployed Centre is down as having paid £20.05p to cover its five delegates and the 6/612 General Workers branch is listed for £5.05p to cover two delegates (though it actually has five), and all from the same Kirkby Unemployment Centre. This reckoning means that their fees cover a total of 28 delegates – they say. But two branches that have between them three delegates seem to have been omitted. If they are added, it still leaves them with 31 delegates.

One result is that the T & G delegation is still not settled. Fortunately I'm told that both Peter Killeen and Ernie Collett are insisting that the union sticks faithfully to the rules of the party. I gather that Peter Killeen has also been told, or may even have discovered for himself, the way in which the T & G has been able to inflate the numbers of its delegates to the Merseyside constituencies way beyond what their membership entitles them to. He's reported to be appalled.

Meanwhile, the national union leaders are still meeting the Liverpool Militants to try to get a deal on the budget that would allow a rise in rates; Reagan and Gorbachov are also trying for peace in our time. I think that the latter have a better chance. I suspect that the Militants have already selected their scapegoat for the blame for what has happened in Liverpool. It's the Labour party. And Neil.

I escaped all this for a short time at the Penal Affairs Group meeting. We discussed a new Private Member's Bill that we intend to introduce in the Lords to tighten up the criteria that have to be satisfied before a custodial sentence can be imposed on a young person. We set up a working party that met under Lord Donaldson, the former Northern Ireland Minister, and which has now produced a draft Bill. This was accepted by the Group and we decided to see the Home Secretary about it and to send it to all the interested organisations for their comments. We also agreed to support the Prior Committee's recommendation for a new independent Prison Disciplinary Tribunal and for a reduction in the maximum loss of remission for a single offence by a prisoner to 120 days. We deferred consideration of whether prisoners should have the right to be legally represented on the Tribunal. I was also instructed to approach the Home Secretary about the threat to prison workshops and on several other matters.

Another good and constructive meeting. Why, I ask myself, can't my constituency party be like this?

Afterwards I sat with Andy Grice on the green leather bench between the Members' and the Central Lobbies. He wanted to do a fairly long interview for a large profile for the *Liverpool Echo*.

'Yes, that's right,' I said for what seemed like the thousandth time, 'I don't live in my constituency.' I was aggressive about it. 'My family comes first. I have no intention of being absentee father . . .'

146

Etc, etc. All over again. I'm weary not just of having to defend myself but also of hearing the same words.

'Yes,' I said in answer to his question about gardening, 'I do have a large garden.' And why shouldn't I have? Why should I be made to feel guilty about it? It's very strange – some of the most left-wing of my party members and certainly of my parliamentary colleagues have acres and more, but somehow what is acceptable in them, like not living in their constituencies, is not acceptable in me.

My colleagues don't help in alleviating the constant barrage of questions about my reselection. Virtually everyone that I speak to, everyone I step into a lift with, sit next to at dinner or in the chamber, begins the conversation with the invariable 'How's your problem?' It's as if I have some terrible disease that's awaiting treatment by a new wonder drug. It's true that the majority, the Tories included, are expressing genuine interest and concern, but even that is boring and annoying. I want to be left alone to nurse my own 'illness'. And they don't really want to know; their eyes go vacant very quickly if I begin to tell the tale. The question has simply become a variant of the 'It's a nice day' opening line.

I also feel that some of my colleagues are enjoying my discomfort. They are pleased that I have been removed, even if only temporarily, as a competitor for office. There are three 'friends' in particular that I dread meeting. As soon as they see me they stride towards me, and then, hands washing and shoulders bent, they cringe, 'How's it going Bob?' It's awful. They want to hear the worst. They're obviously the kind that revel in death and disaster. Of course they're full of sympathy which is probably sincere, but it's sickening and I don't want it. I take extraordinary measures to avoid them.

Even Bryan Gould made me angry. He's a good friend – he must be, to say what he said to me. He came rushing after me as I left the Chamber after Prime Minister's Questions this afternoon and we stood in the 'No' lobby as he waited for a Tory to pass by before speaking.

'How's it going?' he asked, meaning my reselection.

'All right,' I answered. I could tell there was something on his mind. This wasn't just a chat.

'There are a lot of us who want to help you. We *will* help you. You know that, don't you?'

I waited.

'But I do have to ask you a question.' Bryan looked embarrassed.

He stopped again as another Tory sauntered past. 'It's an offensive, an impertinent question, but I have to ask. You won't go and join the SDP when this is all over, if it goes wrong and you don't get reselected?'

'Bryan . . .' I said, putting my hand on his shoulder.

'That's okay,' he said, relieved to have the distasteful duty completed. 'I had to ask.'

I suppose he did. It's a natural suspicion, and one which I know many of my colleagues, even friends like Bryan, will share. There are too many precedents, unfortunately, of ex-Labour MPs who got into trouble with their constituency party, received help from their colleagues, and then left the party and let them down. I shall not join them, though, I know that. Yes, I feel bitter, resentful even. It would be strange if I did not. But I hope that I'm mature and sensible enough to be able to distinguish the shits in my constituency party from the decent members of the Labour party there and elsewhere, and to be able to see the difference between the revolutionary madness that they espouse and the values Neil stands for and that I endorse. In any case, it's my party and it represents my people. I do not feel any affinity for the SDP. I don't think I could be a defector. It's not a role I could easily fit myself to.

In fact, instead of being angry with Bryan for asking the question I felt sorry that he's been put in the position of having to ask it.

Edwina Currie also got it wrong, on another matter. She's the hardline Tory MP for South Derbyshire who rattled a pair of handcuffs in front of a Tory Party Conference. She was ready, she thought, to make another splash at Prime Minister's Question Time today. Already looking round for the anticipated applause, she asked sycophantically, whether the Prime Minister would congratulate the judge who handed out the 'hefty sentences' to the Brixton gang rapists? She obviously expected to be cheered. Instead she was heckled, and not only by the Tories. 'Not long enough,' Jeff Rooker and I shouted. 'Not long enough.' 'Not tough enough,' Thurrock's Oonagh McDonald heckled her. Edwina Currie was visibly rattled and disconcerted, but I suppose that was to be expected. She thinks of herself as being on the right of the Tory party and hard-line on law and order and here she was being heckled by three Labour lefties. Jeff is, of course, the MP who bravely condemned the Handsworth rioters for their lawlessness, even though many of them were his constituents and if not members of then certainly with sympathisers in his constituency party. But then Jeff represents the real Labour party; he knows the difference between right and wrong and he's also prepared to say it in public in his blunt, no-nonsense Brummie fashion.

Wednesday 20th November 1985

Peter Fisher strikes again. He's uncovered another delegate who has not been properly appointed by the branch of the union that he claims to represent. This time it's an ASTMS delegate. The figures now look like this: there are 137 delegates, of whom I must have 69 to win. I still have 66 and ten possibles. And we still have to sort out the T & G.

Peter has a long list of other delegates he still intends to challenge. He's been doing an amazing amount of detective work. Some are not on the electoral register for the address at which they say they live; others appear not to work at the site of the union branch that seems to have affiliated them. It is a laborious process which takes a great deal of time, especially as the enquiries have to be undertaken discreetly for fear that any forewarning will lead to the covering up of the evidence against them. Our experience with the T & G has taught us both a great deal. 'Can we trust them?' is the most frequent question when he or I or Geoff Kneale suggest that approaches for information be made to people that we do not know well.

As for the T & G, I'm told that Bobby Owens has now received a letter from Ernie Collett pointing out that the two branches omitted from the list of branches that the union submitted as taking up their affiliation fee must be included. This means that the union has to start all over again in apportioning its £111 amongst its delegates, and it will have to remove at least three more of them. Which three will it choose? I will be interested to see, especially as I gather that the delegates themselves are arguing about which of them should be dropped. 'The comrades,' I was told, 'have started fighting amongst themselves.' That can't be bad.

According to Bevins in *The Times*, Kenneth Baker, the Secretary of State for the Environment, will if necessary send in commissioners to run Liverpool and oust the Militants if Neil will agree to support the necessary legislation. It will certainly have my support. I feel like saying so publicly but desist only because I don't want to inflame the situation and destroy any strategy and initiative that Jack Cunning-ham and Neil may be engaged in. We can't go on allowing a bunch of political thugs and spivs to hold the local authority workforce to ransom in the way that they are. The Government must govern, otherwise 'mere anarchy is loosed upon the world'. It's responsible for all its citizens and has a duty to ensure that the people of Liverpool are not treated unfairly.

It will be a difficult choice for Neil. He's had a lot of hard decisions to take, but there's no option if the Militants won't accept a rescue along the lines of those that have already been offered to them. It will cause ructions in the party. All the prima donnas will be there looking to see what's in it for them: the Heffers, the Benns, the Skinners will all be posturing and parading. And they'll get a lot out of it, no doubt about that. I'm sure that they're already licking their lips in anticipation of the embarrassment and distress they might be able to cause Neil and the boost they will be able to give to their over-blown egos. But what else can he do? Support the Militants? They're out to destroy both him and the Labour party. Let Liverpool suffer? No, definitely not.

The trouble is that a large number of my colleagues in the parliamentary party and of the national trade union leaders still think that the likes of Hatton and Mulhearn are no different to the rest of us. They think that they will see reason and respond to common sense. They won't.

I emphasised this to Jack Cunningham during the vote on the televising of parliament. We were both in what we thought at the time was the victorious 'Aye' lobby.

'You must be sure,' I insisted, 'that you don't get too enmeshed with them. Don't trust them. They'll rat on any deal. They'll do everything necessary to put the blame elsewhere, and you and Neil have already been measured up and been found to fit the size.'

He understood. It's a pity that more don't – and didn't a long time ago.

Nor, I'm afraid, do all my colleagues understand what is happen-ing to me. I know that many of them believe that my difficulties must be attributable to something that I've failed to do, or to some defect in my character, but I didn't expect them actually to say so to me. Well, they don't, at least not in a straightforward way. They approach the subject by talking about themselves and the way they ensure that they remain on good terms with their constituency parties. It's a surreptitious way of giving me advice, I suppose. It happened tonight at dinner in the Members' Dining Room.

''Course,' said Ron Leighton, the MP for Newham North East, having enquired after my political welfare, 'I always make sure that I send them all Christmas cards. Never miss.' He put his elbow on the crisp white table cloth and rested his chin on his fist.

'Nor me,' Guy Barnett, representing Greenwich, chipped in. Donald Dewar remained silent and glanced sideways at me. I sipped my red wine.

'And I go round trying to get good decent people to become delegates,' Guy added. 'Then I spend hours on the phone making sure that they turn up for meetings and vote the right way.'

I allowed this implied criticism to go on for some time. It was when one of them asked if I held regular surgeries that I exploded.

'Oh come on. What do you think I am? I know all about sending out Christmas cards, being nice to people and organising the votes. I've done it for years. We all do it, for Christ's sake. This is different.'

'I wasn't suggesting that . . .' Ron said conciliatingly.

'Yes, you were, Ron,' I answered. 'You might not be aware of it, but you were. Listen,' I said. 'They control all the Liverpool seats. I don't have to be in trouble. I could go along with them like all the others do and then I'd have no difficulties. But I'll tell you one thing. Sending out Christmas cards isn't the answer.'

I wish it were. They seem to have forgotten how good hardworking MPs like Robin Corbett and Bryan Gould failed to get reselected for their seats after being defeated in the 1979 General Election. Both are good friends of mine but I can say without fear of contradiction that they had both been conscientious and highly competent MPs ever since they were first elected. They also lived in their constituencies. Fortunately for them, they both got selected for seats that they won in 1983 and so are now in Parliament, whereas the candidates that were selected in their places lost.

Later, sitting in a deep green leather armchair in the library, reading John Cole's regular column in the *Listener* and waiting for the vote at midnight on the new board and lodging regulations, I recalled the conversation. It had depressed me. I realised that they did not expect me to survive. I wondered if I would still be here after the next election. I hope so. I love the Commons. Who wouldn't? I like its wide carpeted corridors, its elegant rooms, the massive lobbies and the general feeling of space. I enjoy mooching in the library and dipping into the world's magazines and newspapers, having dinner with friends who are good company and being at the centre of things.

Mind you, we're not always aware that we're at the 'centre of things'. More than once I've rung home to have Jan greet me with something like: 'Wasn't it terrible?'

'What?' I'd say, having no idea what she was referring to.

'The demo.'

'What demo?'

'The one in the House,' she'd say impatiently.

'When?'

'Today. Where are you? You are in the House, I suppose?'

I was, and I had been, probably, since nine-thirty in the morning and would be until ten-thirty in the evening. That's a short day, one of the more civilised ones – unlike today, for instance, when I shall leave for home well after midnight.

She would then tell me about something that I had completely missed even though I was in the building and only a few yards away from where it had occurred. Tuned into Radio 4, Jan gets the news early. We, on the other hand, are rarely in the chamber after Question Time and the two speeches from the Front Benches. Instead we're at the plethora of standing or select committees that now meet most mornings and, afterwards, attending the various party backbench subject groups, the all-party groups or just plain meetings. There are a great many of these.

At the moment I'm spared most of them, but before being appointed to the Shadow Home Office team I carried a pretty onerous load. Besides being chairman of the Penal Affairs Group, I was chairman of the Parliamentary party's Home Office group and of its Civil Liberties group which met weekly. I was a member of the Home Office select committee and of its sub-committee on race relations and immigration, a member of the Home Office sub-committee of the National Executive Committee of the Labour party and on the standing committee that met every morning and evening on Tuesdays and Thursdays to deal with the Police and Criminal Evidence Bill.

They were hectic times: a 15- or 16-hour day was unexceptional. On being appointed to the Front Bench, however, I was required to relinquish all of my committee posts with the exception of the chairmanship of the Penal Affairs Group, which I still hold. It's now the only position that I have. At least it means that for the moment I do not have an obligation to attend a seemingly endless succession of meetings.

This situation will soon change. Naturally, I can't become chairman of the various committees again, or ever go back into the select committee. Other people have taken on the jobs and they must be allowed to get on with them. I will, however, want to serve on a standing committee dealing with legislation. No doubt I shall be on the Public Order Bill Committee and one of the standing committees dealing with the proposed laws on drugs. At the moment, though, it is a quiet time in parliamentary terms; at the beginning of the session none of the standing committees have yet been formed. It's the calm before the storm.

Yet I have to confess that I enjoy being on committees dealing with Bills, just as I revel in Question Time and in debates in the chamber. In the latter two I relish the noise, the heckling, the conflict and the political battle. It's exhilarating. It's also fun. There's something different about the debates in committee – they are, of course, in a smaller and more intimate room, with the other side literally only a yard away. It's not conducive to shouting. Even the members of the public are within spitting distance. But it's more than the nature of the room that determines the character of the discussion. It's usually more structured, more to the point, more concerned with making a case and with changing people's minds than with political point-scoring, though that, naturally, happens too. But there is less of it than in the theatre of the chamber. Moreover, you can actually succeed not only in changing people's minds but in altering the law. The notion that back benchers are powerless or ineffectual is nonsense. There is not a single standing committee of the dozens I've been on where I haven't not succeeded in amending the law, beginning with the amendment to the Finance Bill that effectively exempted war widows pensions from income tax. Of course I was motivated to do that by my mother's experience as a war widow, and particularly my stepfather's account of how he arrived at her home after the war to find her sitting in the cold and dark with me on her knee because she had no money to put in the meter. He'd kicked the table in anger. 'His father's a dead hero,' he said. 'We didn't fight for you to be treated like this.' I felt privileged to have the opportunity all these long years later to make some amends to surviving war widows who had been shabbily treated.

But back to the committees. Even the atmosphere in the long committee corridor on the second floor of the Palace of Westminster is different. It's like a market place, especially during the morning when every one of its two dozen or so committee rooms is probably in use. Lobbyists from all kinds of organisations will be there with their leather briefcases and their plastic folders trying to convince MPs of their case, or providing the already converted with speeches to make and answers to the points made by the opposition. Other MPs will be seated on the dark green leather benches along the walls dictating letters to their secretaries. Some will be speaking on the telephone set in the window alcove on the opposite walls. The lady from the Tea Room will trundle her trolley with an urn of coffee and cheap biscuits from one end to the other. And every so often a policeman will come out of a room, shout, 'Division in number nine,' and the respective MPs will scurry towards the room to vote before the door is locked in their faces.

Yes, I'd miss all that.

Thursday 21st November 1985

The Prescot East branch of my party met tonight in the Labour Club in Shaw Lane, Prescot, and unanimously passed a resolution calling upon the National Executive of the Labour party to undertake an inquiry into the way the constituency party is being run. They have been threatening to do this for some time. Several of them have written letters of complaint about the way the party is being, as they see it, mismanaged. Many of the branch members are amongst those who have been the most disturbed by the way the Militants and their supporters have behaved.

If there is an enquiry, it will probably mean that my reselection will have to be postponed. I've become reconciled to that. In any case it looked as if it would have to be delayed in order for Peter Killeen to have enough time to sort out the T & G delegation. But although I'm philosophical about the whole thing (what else can I be?), I am also slightly disturbed by the additional uncertainty and aggravation that there will be.

Before the resolution was discussed and voted upon we had to empty the small snooker room of the television crews that had located themselves there. I was asked to speak at the branch meeting some time ago. Hearing of the meeting, both Granada TV and ITN asked if they could film it and the chairman agreed. So we all squeezed into the small side room off the main hall, drinks on the tables, the air full of cigarette smoke, and sweated under the television lights.

I decided to make a speech on unemployment and the need to elect a Labour government determined to tackle it, and the danger that we will be prevented from winning an election if we do not first deal with the Militants. Given that the Liverpool Militants are still refusing to accept a deal that will rescue the city and appear to be happy to plunge it and its workforce and people into misery and chaos, the topic seemed to be highly relevant. It has been a long time since I've issued an advance press release of a speech, but this time I did. If I was going to make a sustained attack on Militant, I reasoned, then I might as well ensure that it had the largest possible audience.

So, before leaving the House of Commons for Heathrow and the shuttle to Manchester, I drafted a couple of hundred words and dictated them over the phone to Chris Moncrieff. I said that the Militant Tendency has no place in a democratic socialist party like the Labour party which believes in the rule of law and parliamentary democracy, because its adherents are a Trotskyite conspiracy hell-bent on political confrontation and chaos such as we are currently witnessing in Liverpool. Moreover, it is a separate political organisation. It has its own programme and policies, its own newspaper and holds its own conference. It has a separate and secret organisation, a separate and secret membership, a separate and secret set of full-time political organisers, and its own separate, secret and by all accounts substantial financial resources.

They should have the guts, I said, to get off the back of the Labour party and stand on their own feet. But they won't, because they know that the British people would treat them with the contempt that they deserve, so they hide behind the respectable skirts of the Labour party and besmirch our good name and tarnish our reputation. This has to stop. The electorate will not have confidence in us while we harbour within our midst a nest of agitators and revolutionaries. They have to be expelled. If we do not chuck them out we will not win, or deserve to win, the next election — and we will not then be able to put the unemployed back to work, to eradicate injustice and oppression or protect the sick and disabled. That, I said, is too high a price to pay for the luxury of tolerating Marxist revolutionaries. For the sake of the Labour party they must go now.

It was a little colourful, over the top even. But it was appreciated. All those in the small hot room agreed. How it will come over in the press and on television is another matter, but at least I had the sense to speak quietly and not to rant.

But that was not the end of the matter. I then had to justify myself all over again in an interview for Granada. It was the 'why don't they like you?' syndrome although this time there was a new angle. Geoff Anderson, the reporter, has been investigating the Militant infiltration of the constituency party for a film Granada intend to screen. He has also been working for the *World in Action* team investigating Hatton. He therefore had a great deal of information, much of which was new to me. I can't wait for it to be televised.

Both he and the reporter from ITN went round the room asking people what they thought of me and whether I was a good MP. No-one refused to be interviewed. Indeed, everyone seemed to enjoy the experience, especially as the two reporters competed for the attention of the more forceful and articulate. For a couple of hours the club seemed to be beseiged, with the two reporters rushing from one group of seated and drinking members to another, the cameras, the lights, the sound equipment and the electric cables trailing after them.

It was a good night. I went to bed late with a feeling of a job well done.

Before going to the meeting I conducted a quick survey of the telephone boxes in Prescot. One of my party members, Alyson Birchall, complained to me that when she needed to make an urgent telephone call recently, she had found twelve kiosks without a coin box and unusable. I wrote to British Telecom about the matter. The District General Manager, E. Jackson, replied saying that there had been an unprecedented number of attacks on phones in the Liverpool area in the last year, with over 1000 thefts from pay phones. This, as he pointed out, placed a severe strain on his resources, especially in terms of finding replacement parts. However, he said that in recognition of the difficulties we were experiencing in Prescot he had accelerated the provision of the new payphones and five had been fitted and additional ones were planned.

This didn't satisfy Alyson, and for good reason. The new phones are concentrated in the town centre. She cited the example of old

156

people having to walk a mile to reach a telephone that works. I asked her to do a survey of all the phones in the town, and this showed that nine are out of use and have never been repaired, three have sealed coin boxes and can therefore only be used for emergency calls and that there are three new and operating pay phones in the town centre. She is worried that British Telecom are deliberately withdrawing the public payphone service in the town.

I wrote again to the District Manager giving him the information that Alyson had compiled, saying that I expected the phones to be repaired and that I would inspect the results. He responded by arranging to restore all the payphones to working order, though some would still only provide emergency services access, and for all the sites identified by Alyson to be given priority for the installation of push button payphones.

My quick survey showed that none of these has yet been installed – though to be fair he only promised them by December – and that several of the repaired phones have been subsequently vandalised. It's not Telecom's fault. We're becoming a dirty, violent and uncaring country.

It's evident in the uncaring way in which people deposit litter, and even their household rubbish. It is equally worrying that people are now reluctant to report thieves and vandals to the police. I can't keep asking the Council to repair vandalised houses and British Telecom to repair damaged phone boxes if we're not prepared to do our bit to stop them being vandalised and damaged in the first place. But people don't want to know. They're afraid of retaliation. They withdraw into their own homes and, as with some of the good people in the Labour party, they opt out.

Friday 22nd November 1985

There's no mention of my speech last night in any of today's newspapers, not even the Liverpool *Daily Post*. I was disappointed. I had visions of banner headlines. I was also surprised, especially as I have been inundated in the last few weeks with requests from the press for comments on the antics of the Liverpool Militants. The *Daily Mail* has been particularly insistent, and repeatedly asked me to write a feature article about what the Militants are doing to Liverpool.

They're prepared to run it any day, they say, and to collect it from anywhere, at any time, in any form.

I was tempted to do it. After all, there are things that need to be said, and the fact that they have not been said already is one of the reasons why the Militants have been able to prosper. In the face of their outrageous statements and actions, silence is interpreted as approval, or can certainly be construed as an absence of criticism. But the *Mail* is not exactly the best place to say what needs to be said.

There was at least the consolation of a reasonable article in the *Liverpool Echo* following my interview with Andy Grice. 'Kilroy's Still Here!' it said, and then in a subtitle 'and he's planning to stay'. Andy Grice must have caught me on one of my rare optimistic and confident days. It was an honest account of what I said to him, though it obviously suited him and his story to portray me as a boxer, with the 'gloves off in his fight against Militant'.

Neil's comments were given wide coverage, too. His disowning of the Militants was welcome and overdue, but the *Mail*'s headline – 'Kinnock Will Back Tories Against Hatton' – shows the constraints under which he and the rest of us have to operate. Well, if necessary Neil will have to back the Government: the important thing is that he has said what virtually every Labour MP has been saying privately for months – even those who appear to be enthusiastic supporters of the Militant's tactics. Perhaps we can now go on like this: knowing the difference between right and wrong, and saying clearly which is which.

Moreover, Neil is now talking not only of expelling the Militants from the party but of a 'purge'. At last the message is getting through. I wonder if the contents of my speech leaked out and had anything to do with this. No, of course not. It was his natural anger and distaste for people who, as he said, were in effect holding the Liverpool workforce hostage and tarnishing the good name of the Labour party in the process.

The question that I was asked in the constituency time after time today was 'When are you going to get rid of them?' That is what everyone wants to know. The question was asked by some shop stewards who face the prospect of redundancies. It was said by a local businessman who has been supplying Liverpool Council with goods and is now facing bankruptcy because he has not received his normal payments. It was reiterated yet again by the ordinary Labour voters that fill the streets of Kirkby and, indeed, the borough of Knowsley.

But it's not just the Militants, or those in Liverpool, who are causing us trouble. We also have them in London and elsewhere. In London they are now refusing the police access to schools. According to an answer to a question that I tabled on the subject, there are 21 schools within the area of the Inner London Education Authority which refuse to allow an educational input by the police. This is stupid and should not be tolerated – no wonder we're seen as being anti-police. All the hard work that is done at a national level by Neil and people like Gerald Kaufman is destroyed at a stroke by left-wing bigots in local government.

Saturday 23rd and Sunday 24th November 1985

Being in the constituency most of Thursday and Friday meant that I had literally masses of letters and phone messages to deal with. Sarah had left them at home for me. They occupied most of Saturday, including the evening, and a fair part of Sunday. This is the side of an ordinary MP's everyday life that people do not see.

But it was an exciting two days. It looks as if the Liverpool saga is coming to an end. Already the Militants have climbed down, humiliated, and accepted that they will have to set a legal budget after all – and the best of it is that the surrender was forced on them by their own district Labour party. Naturally the Hattons are out in force saying that it's all Neil's fault, but I think that by now everyone can see through his vicious and spiteful ranting. The people know the truth. They know that they've been used and manipulated.

Better still is that Neil is now reputed to be determined that the Liverpool Militants should be expelled from the party and he's canvassing support for a motion to this effect to be passed at Wednesday's meeting of the National Executive. About time too. It should have happened a long time ago. If only Michael Foot had taken the action that several of us consistently and repeatedly pressed upon him before the disastrous 1983 general election.

Natasha and her four girl friends went off in a blustery wind on Saturday to support their football team. It doesn't seem all that long ago that Jan was coming to watch me. Indeed, we met when she was only a little older than Natasha is now – it feels as if it were only a couple of years ago.

We also collected the puppy, or rather Jan and Natasha did. Dominic still effects to be uninterested and I had too much work to get through. She's smaller than I expected. It's hard to believe that she will grow into a dog big and powerful enough to swim the Thames at Maidenhead where it's wide and swift. She'll have to be house-trained, and she will also start all the ruddy business of chewing things up. I don't know why we do it, especially as the kids are now grown up. Jan and Natasha are treating her as if she were a baby.

This evening, after I'd written my column for *Time Out*, I escaped with Joan Didion and *Democracy*. I read the first eighteen or so pages, could not understand a thing of what was supposed to be happening, re-read them and then literally could not put the book down until I finished it. An extraordinary novel. She has a strange style that takes a great deal of getting used to, but when you've adjusted to it it's irresistible. I found that I was having conversations with myself in the fashion of the book: if I'm not careful I shall start writing like that. It was Joan Didion and her *Run River* that caused me to drive Jan and the kids along the wide levees of the Sacramento River from San Francisco to the capital of California in 1978. It was an exhilarating and wonderful journey.

The real Liverpool also won, beating Birmingham with goals from Rush and Walsh, and Manchester United lost to near-bottom Leicester. We're only two points behind now. I said that we'd claw our way back up, didn't I? Just like the real Labour party is doing.

Monday 25th November 1985

It looks as if some decisions will be taken at Wednesday's meeting of the National Executive. Besides having to decide what to do about the Liverpool Militants it will be required to determine whether or not to allow my reselection to proceed. The chances are that it will be postponed. The Prescot East branch of my party has already called for an inquiry. Now, according to Peter Fisher, the officers of the Knowsley Village branch have also written in support of Prescot East. Together, these two wards account for over 60 per cent of the membership of the constituency party, so they should be listened to.

In addition, Peter tells me that several individual party members have written to the general secretary, Larry Whitty, complaining about the way in which the constituency party is run and calling for an investigation.

There is interesting news, too, from the regional office of the Labour party in Manchester. They have still not managed to agree with the T & G on the number of delegates that it is entitled to. It's getting late, because nominations close this Thursday, 28th November. There are just three candidates: myself, Tony Mulhearn and Keva Coombes. Jim Lloyd failed to get nominated. Indeed, on several occasions he did not receive a single vote. The meeting to decide the shortlist of those who will be invited to attend the selection conference on 10th December is next Tuesday, 3rd December. By the time they vote on the shortlist, all the delegates' credentials must have been verified; I don't think that it can be done. Apart from the muddle – that's a nice neutral word – with the T & G, there are other delegates whose right to attend the meetings we've challenged and who have not yet been cleared. They've no doubt been put to one side by Peter Killeen while he tussles with the T & G, but they have all got to be dealt with. They can't be done in a rush, and I'll insist that they're done thoroughly. If nothing else, Peter Fisher's efforts deserve that.

In these circumstances the least the National Executive should do is to postpone the selection. However, on the evidence that is now available to the national officials, it should also hold an investigation, but that decision will presumably, depend upon what it decides to do about Liverpool. And that in turn depends on whether Neil has enough votes. Let us hope that this time he has.

Before leaving the House just before seven tonight I looked in the chamber to see what was happening. It was virtually empty. A debate on agriculture on a Monday evening and no vote at ten o'clock are reasons enough for a light attendance, but nevertheless it's worrying that there are so few members, of either side, prepared to be in the chamber listening to their colleagues. Of course, the proliferation of committees, especially the high-powered select committess, imposes a considerable extra burden of work on members and takes them out of the chamber, but it's a pity that in the process it is losing its character. Nor indeed do members go to the chamber to listen to the 'star' speakers nowadays. I remember when Michael Foot's name was announced on the TV screen in the

Member's Tea Room during the debate on Nato just a month after he had resigned as leader of the party. No-one moved. A recent leader of the party, speaking on an important subject closely related to what was said to have been a major cause of our election defeat, and no-one could be bothered to go and hear him.

'Come on,' Brian Sedgemore said to me. 'Let's give the old man some support.'

I followed him into the chamber where Michael, half bent sideways as if crippled, was addressing an almost empty chamber from the backbenches. Only John Silkin, then the Shadow Defence Secretary, was on the front bench. All the Tories present were busily talking to each other and, to tell the truth, Brian and I also spent the time gossiping.

Tuesday 26th November 1985

I've been depressed and miserable all day at the thought of having to go to what I know will be another vile and vicious meeting of my management committee tonight. I don't feel like attending. I have good reason not to because there's a vote in the Commons tonight, but I know that I must be in Knowsley with those who are fighting the Militants and need the moral support of my presence and my verbal help when I'm allowed to speak. I also have to face the music for what I said in the Michael Cockerell film and since. There are, I know, resolutions from all the Militant-dominated branches condemning me. It should be entertaining.

The media doesn't help to alleviate my depression. Today alone, in the relatively short time that I was at home this morning before leaving for the Commons, I had calls from ITN, Channel 4, *Newsnight*, TV am, Granada TV and the BBC. They all want to arrange to interview me.

Some of them want to talk to me about the problems of my own reselection and they want to interview me in Knowsley, now, this very minute. As always with television they expect you to drop everything you are doing and attend to their requests. They're surprised when I refuse. They're not used to people saying no.

Others, like TV am, want me to make a comment on the Liverpool Militants that they can screen both before and after the NEC meeting tomorrow which will discuss the possibility of having an inqiury into the affairs of the Liverpool District Labour party. These I also refused. I've turned most of them down because they're logistically impossible. I can't be in two places at once – though they do not seem to appreciate it. I certainly can't get from Knowsley in time to be on TV am in the early hours of the morning tomorrow, and even if I could I wouldn't do it. It's too tiring. It would destroy tomorrow as an effective working day. There's a great deal that I have to do, especially as the media took up the morning I had set aside for other things that will now have to wait until tomorrow.

I've also refused because it may not be wise for me to be on every television programme just before the NEC meet to make a decision on my reselection. I may well be wrong, but my judgement is that I might irritate people whose support, and perhaps even votes, I may need tomorrow.

Even so, the telephone conversations take up a great deal of time. The reporters all seem to need to be taken slowly and carefully through the story, to have it all explained to them right from the very beginning. As most are not political reporters, the educational task that I'm confronted with is more difficult because all the nuances have to be explained, the consequences and the implications highlighted. It's a weary process. It's also demoralising constantly to have to answer these perfectly proper but highly personal and wounding questions. The wound is never allowed a moment to heal – there's always another phone call, another innocent questioning voice carefully peeling it open again.

At least in the constituency there's no messing about. They got the knives out straight away. There were a lot of them in evidence tonight. The meeting began with a row when the brave and decent Mike Murphy, a district councillor and one of the signatories of the letter supporting me that *The Times* refused to publish, asked why the letter from Ernie Collett sent to all constituency party secretaries in the North West on the subject of Militant had not been read out at the last meeting. He had a copy of it and he read parts of it out, when he could be heard above the heckling. The letter said that in accordance with the decision of Annual Conference, the constituency party must not invite Militant speakers to their meetings, make donations to their fighting fund or provide facilities for the sale of *Militant*. The constituency party has already, of course, invited and heard Tony Mulhearn. So have several of the branches, probably all of them that are dominated by Militant. As for the newspapers, the chairman himself used to sell it but he seems now to have delegated that responsibility to an acolyte who stands in the corridor of the Kirkby Unemployed Centre advertising its nasty message before and after meetings.

I can't be bothered to go into details of who said what to whom in the ensuing slanging match. Suffice it to say that during one of the tirades directed against people like Mike Murphy, Dave Kerr, the 'impartial' press secretary, stood up, pointed his finger in the manner of all Militants and screamed that Frank Marsden was an 'animal and arsehole'. I wrote the words down on the back of the minutes of the last meeting as he spoke them from the front row. The words accurately convey a flavour of the meeting and of how elderly and respected people like Frank are vilified and abused. The wonder is not that people like Dave Kerr have taken over the Labour party; the wonder is that decent people like Mike Murphy, Peter Fisher and, above all, the older members like Frank and Muriel Marsden and Frances and Harry Bailey still bother to turn up.

But of course the main focus of the abuse was me, as it always is. I sometimes think that my role at these meetings is to be an Aunt Sally. I'm here as a representative of all that they despise and hate, the object on which to vent their anger and spite.

There were, as I've said, several resolutions affecting me, and it was clear that this was the highlight of the evening. Business had obviously been expedited so that they could leave plenty of time for my 'trial'. It was clear too that the movers and seconders of the resolutions and the speaker in the debate had all been selected beforehand, no doubt at the secret meeting that they now hold in The Kingfisher pub in Bewley Drive, Kirkby.

Unfortunately the speeches weren't all that coherent. Nor, strangely, did they look directly at me when they spoke. They seemed to want to get to the vote and get it over with, but I insisted on speaking in my defence.

The charges, as I summarised them, were: I had canvassed for votes – I hadn't, so I denied it; I had threatened to hold a by-election – I said I was 'considering it'; I had alleged that the Kirkby Unemployed Centre was where the Militants met – I reiterated that I believed this to be true; I had called for the expulsion of Militant supporters from the Labour party – I pleaded guilty and repeated the offence; I had directed lies and insults at the chairman – I insisted that everything I said had been true, that I retracted nothing, and that if I'd known then what I know now I would have said much more; and that I had said that the meetings of the party were disorderly and that people were threatened and intimidated.

'But they are,' I said. 'It's happened again tonight. It's been disorderly. It's been disruptive. People have been sworn at, abused and threatened. It's true.' They didn't say a word, not a single word. And they remained silent when I pleaded guilty to saying that additional delegates had come on to the management committee for the T & G and that yes, I had said that I wanted the party disbanded. 'I plead guilty to that. I said it. I said it because I believe that the party has been mismanaged and ought to be disbanded and reconstituted.'

I don't know what they expected me to say – I don't think they really knew themselves. Some of them obviously thought that faced with their resolutions, their speeches and their votes of condemnation, I would retract, that I would find, as others have done, that black was white after all. Bugger that. As Neil said to Jan when he and Glenys were at our house for dinner, 'You've got to look at yourself in the mirror the next morning.' And it's true, you have. Like all politicians, like everyone else, I've made compromises and deals, of course – that's life. But I haven't told lies, I haven't voted for something that I don't believe in, and I've never pretended to be somebody that I'm not. I'm not ashamed of anything that I've done politically – except perhaps that I didn't support Peter Fisher more fully when he exposed some of the practices of Knowsley Council, and that I didn't speak out on Scargill and the Militants earlier. But at least I don't creep to the likes of them. When people like me do the bidding of people like them then the game really is up.

Mind you, they can be amusing. One of them, in moving the resolution condemning me, quoted from my *Time Out* column. He said that I attacked fellow Labour MPs like Brian Sedgemore who had been campaigning about the scandals in the City. The truth is that, with Brian's knowledge and consent, because he's a mate, I wrote a humorous piece about the activities of him and Dale Campbell-Savours, the MP for Workington. I said that the 'odd couple are back', and called them 'The best pair of political muggers in the business'. 'Most days,' I wrote 'you can find them in the slummy end of the Tea Room, talking behind their hands, or closeted together whispering in the darker corners and the furthest recesses of the Library, planning another jape. Nor are they short of targets. Besides the present kerfuffle over the Johnson Matthey

Bank, others have included British Oxygen and, of course, the Oman – Mark Thatcher saga. 'Results so far? Dale banned from the House for two days and Brian for five.'

What my accuser objected to tonight was that I had called them 'political muggers'. And where had the phrase come from? From Dale. 'Don't forget,' he said when I told him what I was doing and asked him to remind me of all the 'campaigns' that he and Brian had been on, 'don't forget to call us the best pair of political muggers in the business.' And now the humourless and small-minded were using it as yet another reason to attack me. I smiled. They didn't.

Mind you, they weren't the only ones: Eric Heffer took the same view. During Question Time he waddled into the chamber, plonked himself alongside Dale, folded his arms across his chest, put a hand across the corner of his mouth and said 'Psst.'

Dale was startled.

'Have you seen *Time Out*?'

Dale shook his head.

'There's a bitter attack on you in it written by Kilroy-Silk. It's in the library.'

Dale started to laugh.

I've already written this up as a paragraph for my next column. I've told Dale that he will have to do a 'Psst' to Heffer, and he can't wait.

But it's interesting, isn't it, how some people also can't wait to see you in trouble and, if need be, will help to put you there?

Wednesday 27th November 1985

It's been a long day. It began in the dark on icy and dangerous roads in Knowsley and ended in uncertainty in London. Throughout the day at the House of Commons I and others awaited news from the meeting of the NEC, but it was never forthcoming. It seemed as if they would be forever discussing the problems of Liverpool and the little local difficulty in Knowsley.

I had anticipated that we would have news by lunchtime. Relaxed, strangely confident, I devoted the morning to dealing with my correspondence and making phone calls on behalf of constituents. I even managed to research the subject for my *Police Review* article that I will need to write tomorrow. I shall write about Gwyneth

Dunwoody's campaign to get tougher sentences imposed on rapists. She has a good case. Although the maximum sentence now available to the courts for rape and attempted rape is life imprisonment, only six of those sentenced for rape in 1984 were actually given life. More disturbing is that the average length of prison sentences for rape was between two and five years. That's not enough, and Gwyneth looks like getting it lengthened.

Still no news at lunchtime, except that they were still in session. As I sat in a green armchair in the Tea Room with a sardine salad every Labour MP who entered asked the same question: 'Any news from the NEC?' Not, you understand, because they wanted to know what was to happen in Knowsley. Most of them were probably unaware that it was even on the agenda. But, like the rest of the political world, they wanted to know about Liverpool. Was Neil taking them on? That was the real issue, though it was rarely put in that form. No-one asked the question that was at the front of their mind: are we going to have a civil war in the party?

Groups of members, Tories included, gathered round the Press Association tape in the wide Library corridor. Still no news. I went up to my small room in the Upper Committee Corridor (North) to write an article on the Data Protection Act that had been commissioned by *Accountancy*. I prepared the material for my article for *Police Review* and even jotted down some preliminary ideas for my *Time Out* column. There was still no news when I finished, nor when I left the Chamber after questions to go to the small room with lead-lined windows off the cavernous Westminster Hall to meet the delegates from Liverpool University's Association of University Teachers who were complaining about the cuts in the grants to universities and the holding down of their own pay.

By the time that Jan collected me to drive to the Mermaid Theatre it was clear that a major row was in progress in the National Executive of the party. We went to the first night of Adam Faith's *Cats Down an Alley*. He rang, belatedly, a few days ago, asking if we'd like a couple of tickets. 'Why not?' I said. 'Sure, let's go. Can we have four tickets?' Joyce Hopkirk and Bill Lear accompanied us. We joined up with Michael and Mary Parkinson and, at the party in the theatre's bar afterwards, with Clare Rayner, the *Sunday Mirror* gossip columnist Chris Hutchins, Sebastian Coe and countless others, most of whom wanted to know what had been decided in Walworth Road about the Liverpool Militants.

'Hadn't you better ring someone up?' Jan asked.

'No.' I didn't want to.

She and Joyce expressed surprise at my apparent lack of interest or anxiety.

'Aren't you even curious?' Jan asked.

'No.'

'He knows. That's why,' Joyce said. She smiled conspiratorially and put her lovely arm around my shoulders. 'He already knows, don't you?'

'He doesn't,' Jan said flatly.

Did I know? I asked myself. No, I didn't. And by then I didn't care either. Whatever happens, it will never be the same again. I can't go back to yesterday. The fun has been taken out of politics for me, at least for now, and I regret that and resent it. I've also become less fun, or so my mother and kids tell me, and I think they're right.

I am resigned to defeat and political oblivion and the adjustment to a new life. It can't be any worse.

POSTSCRIPT

Liverpool Football Club who were nine points behind Manchester United at the top of the League at the beginning of this diary, won both the League Championship and the FA Cup.

Peter Fisher was, as anticipated, deselected on 12 February 1986 when nine members of the Beyga family turned up at the Ward meeting and voted for their relative, Gerry Beyga.

Peter Fisher subsequently stood in the Council election on 8 May as a "Labour against the Militant" Candidate. He won by 1,572 votes to 701 for Mr Beyga, the biggest majority of any candidate.

Tony Mulhearn was expelled from the Labour Party by the NEC on 22 May 1986.

Derek Hatton was expelled from the Labour Party by the NEC on 12 June 1986.

Keva Coombes was selected as a candidate for Hyndburn, and the author was therefore the only candidate left nominated for Knowsley North. By then, however, his enthusiasm for politics had been destroyed.

In July 1986 he announced that he would be resigning from Parliament in the autumn.

INDEX

Accountancy 167
Aldritt, Walter 129
Anderson, Geoff 156
Archer, Jeffrey (vice-chairman of Tory party; novelist) 144
Ashton, Joe (MP for Bassetlaw) 31, 131
Ashton, Maggie 31
ASTMS 16, 60, 138, 149
Atkinson, Norman (MP for Tottenham) 67
Atyeo, Don (editor, *Time Out*) 120
AUEW 57
Avebury, Lord 70, 102

Bailey, Frances 58, 83, 94, 164
Bailey, Harry 164
Baker, Kenneth (Secretary of State for the Environment) 14, 45, 149
Barker, Kent (BBC radio reporter) 24
Barlow, Helen 49
Barlow, Sir William (chairman BICC) 44
Barnet, Guy 151
Barnicoat, Tom 28
Barron, Kevin (MP for Rother Valley) 105
Beaumont-Dark, Tony 106
Beaver (LSE newspaper) 88
Benn, Tony 2, 17, 26, 33, 34, 41, 73
Bennett, Andrew 41
Bevins, Tony (political correspondent of *The Times*) 28, 34, 68, 125; on the author's reselection 3, 64, 109, 123; on Militants 18, 133, 149
Beyga, Gerry*
Beyga, Tony 37, 57
BICC (Prescot) 44–5, 52–4, 88–9, 124
Biffen, John 136
Birchall, Alyson 156–7
Birk, Baroness 70
Birmingham 19–20, 29

Blackstock, Stuart 20, 21
Blakelock, PC 59
Bournemouth Conference (1985) 15, 23–6, 27–33, 35, 38–9, 40, 79, 83, 163
Bower, Tom 89
Boyd, William 142
Boyes, Roland (MP) 38–9
Boyle, Jimmy 61
Bragg, Melvyn 93
Breakfast Time (BBC TV) 47
British Telecom 156–7
Brittan, Leon 90, 102
Broadwater Farm Estate (Tottenham) 58–9, 107
Brown, Dave 82–3
Brown, Gordon 41
Burne, Jerome 120
Burnett, Alistair 100
Butcher, John (Industry Minister) 45
Byrne, Tony 17

Cadbury Trust 103
Callaghan, Jim 40, 41–2
Callan, Paul 144
Callil, Carmen 140
Campaign Group 41
Campbell-Savours, Dale (MP for Workington) 165–6
Canavan, Dennis 105
Cantril Farm 40, 43, 45
Cartwright, John 105–6, 122
Cavadino, Paul (clerk to the Penal Affairs Group) 20, 21, 103
Ceremony of Innocence, The 42, 59, 70
Chloe (the author's dog) 64, 86, 90, 94, 96
Clark, Alan (Paymaster General) 143
Clements, Dick 71
Clwyd, Ann (MP for Cynon Valley) 38–9
Cockerell, Bridget 138

Cockerell, Michael (BBC TV reporter) 75, 79, 89, 97–8, 122, 124, 138; film on the author 18–19, 28, 35–6, 37–8, 44, 52–4, 57–8, 64, 72–3, 94–6, 162
Cocks, Michael 67–8, 106
Cole, John 151
Collett, Ernie (Labour Party regional organiser) 121–2, 137, 146, 149, 163
Concannon, Don (MP for Mansfield) 31
Conference of Prison Chaplains 131
Cook, Robin 41
Coombes, Keva (Leader of Merseyside County Council) 4–5, 37, 161
Co-operative Party 9, 76
Corbett, Robin (MP for Birmingham Erdington) 115, 151
Corbyn, Jeremy (MP for Islington North) 95–6, 98, 99–100, 106, 108, 113
Coren, Alan 93, 118, 140
Coren, Anne 140
Country Living 130
Courtaulds factory (Aintree) 45
Cowans, Harry 50
Crick, Michael 35
Criminal Justice Act (1982) 101
Cunningham, Jack 14–15, 41–2, 70, 150
Cure, Ken (AUEW member of NEC) 34
Currie, Edwina (MP for South Derbyshire) 148

Daily Express 118, 122, 144
Daily Mail 49, 144, 157–8
Daily Mirror 30–1, 34, 50, 106, 144
Daily Star 31
Daily Telegraph 115, 118
Davenport, Peter 109–110
David, Baroness 70, 102
Davis, Anne 133
Davis, Terry (MP for Birmingham, Hodge Hill) 133
Day, Sir Robin 24–5, 118–20, 122
Dempster, Nigel 144
Dewar, Donald 151

Didion, Joan 160
Dimbleby, David 95–6
Donaldson, Lord 70, 102, 146
Drabble, Phil 130
Dubs, Alf (MP for Battersea) 41, 69
Dunford, Philip 48
Dunwoody, Gwyneth 166–7

East, Guy 11–12, 64, 114
Ebert, Jake 114
Edmonds, John (general secretary of GMBATU) 144
EEPTU 60, 76
Elliott, Mike 114
Evans, Ioan 38, 41
Evans, John (MP for St Helens North) 76, 99, 104, 134
Evans, Moss (general secretary of T & G) 42

Fabian Conference News 42
Fabian Society 9, 76
Faith, Adam 167
Faithful, Baroness 102
Falkender, Marcia 114
Faulds, Andrew (MP for Warley East) 133
Fazakerley Engineering Works (Kirkby) 108
Field, Frank (MP for Birkenhead) 4, 36, 67, 71, 76, 95–6; supports the author 112, 122, 127, 128–9, 136–7
Fields, Terry (Militant MP for Liverpool Broadgreen), 6–7, 24–5, 36, 73, 75, 116, 129
Fisher, Jan 110
Fisher, Peter 8, 37, 74, 76, 79, 91, 110, 111, 116, 127, 137, 160–1, 164; investigates management committee delegates 11, 16–17, 21, 22, 55–7, 59, 61, 64, 97, 136, 149, 161; in Cockerell's film 95; letter to The Times 129–30; and Knowsley Council 139, 165, 169

Fletcher, Tim (Margaret Thatcher's private secretary) 46
Foot, Michael 33, 35, 159, 161–2
Fowler, Norman 85

Fraser, Nick 133
Freud, Clement 131

Gallagher, Tom 113
Gardner, Sir Edward (MP for
  South Fylde) 61
General & Municipal Workers
  Union (GMBATU) 57, 60, 83,
  120, 123, 135
Golding, John 70
Goldman, Andrew and Ye Ye 113
Gordon, Angela 144
Gould, Bryan 40, 147–8, 151
Gould, Jill 40
Granada TV 47, 54–5, 61, 155–6,
  162
Grant, Bernie (leader of Haringay
  Borough Council) 59, 67
Greer, Germaine 34
Grice, Andy 24, 71–2, 115, 146–7,
  158
Guardian, The 6, 106, 113, 118,
  122, 123, 128, 134
Gummer, John (junior Minister of
  Agriculture) 112

Haines, Joe 144
Hamilton, Jimmy (MP for Central
  Fife) 105
Hamilton, John (Militant leader of
  Liverpool City Council) 25, 128
Handsworth riots 148–9
Hanley, Jeremy (MP) 70
Hardwick, Mike (Managing
  Director, Time Out) 120
Harman, Harriet (MP for Peckham)
  34, 41
Harris, Lord 102
Hattersley, Roy 69
Hatton, Derek (deputy leader,
  Liverpool City Council) 8, 25, 34,
  37, 59, 95, 107, 134, 144, 150,
  156; News of the World article on
  17–18, 51; conflict with Kinnock
  117, 158, 159, 169
Healey, Denis 26, 70, 131, 141
Heath, Duncan 12
Heathcoat-Amory, David 105
Heffer, Eric 23–4, 26–7, 34, 61, 73,
  76, 116, 166; and the author's

anti-Militant campaign 132, 133,
  141
Hennessy, Peter 54–5
Herlitz, Esther 40
Heseltine, Michael 40
Hickey, William 144
Hillmore, Peter 144
Hindley, Myra 20
Hogan, James (BBC TV producer) 24
Hogg, Douglas (MP) 70
Holmes, Doris 58
Hooley, Frank (former MP) 1–2, 3
Hopkirk, Joyce 140, 144, 167–8
Howard League for Penal Reform
  102
Howell, Denis 69
Hoyle, Doug (MP for Warrington
  North) 33
Hughes, Bob 41
Hughes, David (Labour Party
  national agent) 100–1
Hughes, Sean (MP for Knowsley
  South) 4, 71, 76, 106, 126–7
Hughes, Tricia 127
Hunt, Lord 70, 102
Hunter, Harry (Managing Director
  BICC, Prescot) 44, 53
Hurd, Douglas (Home Secretary) 71,
  103
Hutchins, Chris 167
Hutchinson, Lord 102
Hygena factory (Kirkby) 45

Independent Radio News 115
Ingham, Bernard (Margaret
  Thatcher's press secretary) 48
ITN 124–5, 155–6, 162

Jackson, E. (District General
  Manager, British Telecom) 156–7
Jackson, Robert 122–3
Jackson, Ruth 11, 64, 114, 133
Jarrett, Mrs Cynthia 58
Jenkin, Patrick (Secretary of State for
  the Environment) 7–8, 14, 47,
  48–9, 62
Jenkins, Clive (general secretary
  ASTMS) 31
Jenkins, Roy 105–6

Jones, Barry (MP for Alyn and
   Deeside) 70
Jones, Graham 115
Jones, Steve 114
Joseph, Keith 45

Kagan, Lord 70
Kaufman, Gerald 40, 67, 70, 159
Kavanagh, Dennis (Professor of
   Politics) 54–5
Keays, Sara 41, 118
Kelly, Mick 124, 127
Kerr, Dave (Militant; Knowsley
   North press officer) 57, 84, 97,
   109–10, 113, 123, 129, 164
Killeen, Peter (Labour Party assistant
   regional organiser) 1, 10–11, 82;
   investigates management
   committee delegates 16, 23, 65–6,
   91, 97, 116–17, 120, 121, 134–5,
   146, 154, 161
Kilroy Mrs (the author's mother)
   19, 77–8, 86, 87, 88, 96, 153, 168
Kilroy, John (the author's stepfather)
   87–8, 127, 136, 153
Kilroy, Madeline (the author's half-
   sister) 77–8, 87
Kilroy-Silk, Dominic (the author's
   son) 12, 64, 86, 90–1, 94, 108,
   114, 142, 160; and the author's
   reselection battle 11, 119, 141,
   168
Kilroy-Silk, Jan (the author's wife)
   18, 33, 74, 116, 117, 121, 130,
   140, 142, 143, 165; and the
   author's reselection battle, 1, 5–6,
   11, 98, 110–11, 168; Tuscan
   holiday 11–12; discusses politics
   15, 99, 119, 131–2, 152; at
   Bournemouth Conference 24, 27,
   28, 29, 30–1, 32, 39, 43; family
   life 42, 51, 52, 64, 77–8, 86,
   90–1, 92–3, 94, 108, 114, 125–6,
   127, 159–60; and Cockerell's film
   64, 94, 96; on the author's
   Shadow Ministerial resignation 66,
   68, 115; and the author's Time
   Out diary 141
Kilroy-Silk, Natasha (the author's
   daughter) 12, 50–1, 64, 88, 90,

92–3, 108, 114, 141, 142,
   159–60; and the author's
   reselection
   battle 11, 168
King, Tom (Secretary of State for
   Employment) 49
Kinnock, Glenys 33, 41, 165
Kinnock, Neil 26, 27, 47, 59, 141,
   148, 165; and the author's
   Shadow Ministerial resignation 5,
   66, 68, 71, 85–6, 115, 118; anti-
   Militants 15, 113, 119, 120, 158,
   159; anti-Militants Conference
   speech 23–4, 25, 28, 35, 58, 79,
   83, 84–5, 139; other Conference
   speeches 29, 31–3, 40–1; and
   Liverpool Militants 62, 85, 91–2,
   106–7, 149–50, 159, 161, 167;
   Shadow Cabinet 68–9; attacked
   by Militants 80, 83–4, 117, 146;
   and the author's reselection battle
   123, 128, 132, 136–7
Kirkby 45, 46–50, 108, 110, 143
Kirkby Labour Club 80
Kirkby Unemployed Centre 36, 72,
   79, 95, 145, 164
Kneale, Frances (Mayor of
   Knowsley) 17, 89, 111, 124, 126,
   138–9
Kneale, Geoff (the author's
   voluntary agent) 11, 17, 46, 79,
   89, 91, 111, 138–9, 149
Kneale, Rita 48, 111
Knowsley: unemployment and
   housing problems 19, 45–9, 63,
   74, 139, 143
Knowsley Council 4, 51, 109,
   142–3, 165
Knowsley North Labour Party 80–1,
   160–1; reselection of MP 1, 3–6,
   8, 10, 16, 21, 154, 160, 161;
   management committee 2, 9–10;
   Militants in 2–3, 8–10, 59–61,
   79–84, 97–8, 163–5, see also
   Militant Tendency; delegates
   investigated 16–17, 21–3, 36, 97,
   see also Fisher, Peter; Killeen, Peter
Knowsley South constituency 4
Knowsley Village Labour Party 54,
   57–8, 160

Labour Against the Militant 169
Labour Friends of Israel 39
Labour Party: north-west regional
    headquarters 97, 121–2, 136, 142,
    161, see also Collett, Ernie;
    Killeen, Peter
Labour Party Annual Conferences
    40–2; (1985) 15, 23–6, 27–33,
    35, 38–9, 40, 79, 83, 163
Lamond, James (MP) 105
Lawler, Frank 139
Lawler, Joe (Militant; vice-chairman
    Knowsley North Labour Party)
    59–61, 84, 95, 97, 120
Lawrence, Sarah (the author's
    secretary) 19, 44, 47, 87, 88, 131,
    137, 142, 159
Lear, Bill 140, 167
Leighton, Ron (MP for Newham
    North East) 151
Life Sentence Prisoners (Penal Affairs
    Group) 102
Litherland, Bob (MP for Manchester
    Central) 105
Liverpool City Council, 8, 17, 25, 51,
    62, 149, 158; and Kinnock 23, 85;
    Militants employed by 60, 95;
    rescue of 123, 150; see also
    Liverpool Militants
Liverpool Daily Post 24, 71–2, 122,
    157
Liverpool District Labour Party 163
Liverpool Echo 6, 24, 71–2, 112,
    115, 146, 158
Liverpool F.C. 19, 51, 62, 76, 93,
    114, 125, 140, 160, 169
Liverpool Militants 12, 14, 17–18,
    26, 36–7, 62–3, 74, 117, 146,
    155; and Kinnock 23, 35, 85,
    91–2, 149–50, 158, 159; BICC
    shop stewards afraid of 52–4; and
    NEC 119, 159, 160, 161, 162–3,
    166; see also Liverpool City
    Council
Livingstone, Ken 47, 143
Lloyd, Jim (Leader of Knowsley
    Council) 4–5, 37, 161
Lloyd, Tony (MP for Stretford) 87
Longford, Lord 69–70, 102
Loyden, Eddie (Militant MP for

Liverpool Garston) 24–5, 76, 129
Luce, Richard (Arts Minister) 142–3

McCluskey, Len (T & G political
    liaison officer) 121
McDonald, Oonagh 148
McGinley, Jim (Militant chairman of
    Knowsley North Labour Party) 8,
    49–50, 95, 124, 127, 164; as
    chairman 82–3, 84; resolution for
    expulsion of 132
McManus, James (journalist) 138
Macmillan, Michael 124–5
McNamara, Kevin (MP for Kingston
    upon Hull) 41, 133
McSorley, Phil (T & G delegate) 16,
    56–7, 100, 121–2
Mail on Sunday, The 114, 127
Mailer, Norman 141–2
Manchester United F.C. 19, 51, 62,
    76, 93, 114, 125, 140, 160, 169
Marsden, Frank (former MP) 94,
    129, 164
Marsden, Muriel 58, 94, 164
Masham, Baroness 102
Maxwell, Ghislane 31, 144
Maxwell, Robert 31, 144
May, Doreen (editor, Police Review)
    121
Maynard, Joan (MP for Sheffield
    Brightside) 33
Meacher, Michael (MP for Oldham
    West) 69, 99–100
Mellor, David (junior Home Office
    Minister) 89–90
Merseyside: unemployment 45, 49,
    60, 74, 139, 143
Merseyside Cooperative
    Development Agency 109
Merseyside County Council 142–3
Merseyside Group of Labour MPs
    3–4
Merseyside Residuary Body 143
Midweek (BBC TV programme) 42
Mikardo, Ian (MP for Bow and
    Poplar) 105–6
Militant (M. Crick) 35
Militant (newspaper) 57, 163–4
Militant Tendency 24–5, 27, 54,
    62–3, 72, 138–9, 158, 159; in

Militant Tendency – *cont.*
Knowsley North 2–3, 8–10,
16–17, 56–7, 59–61, 79–84,
94–5, 97–8, 163–4; conflict with
the author, 4–6, 7, 35–6, 21–3,
65, 71–2, 75–6, 109–10, 116,
155–6, 162, 164–5; and Kinnock
23–4, 28, 35, 146, 158; *see also*
Liverpool Militants
Mitchell, Austin (MP for Great
Grimsby) 33
Molloy, Mike (editor, *Daily Mirror*)
143–4
Moncrieff, Chris 115, 155
Montgomery, Dave (editor, *News of
the World*) 17, 51
Morrison, Peter 47, 49
Mulhearn, Tony (Militant President
of Liverpool Labour Party) 25, 60,
82, 94, 150, 163; and Knowsley
North 4, 57, 72, 119–20, 124,
127, 129, 161, 169
Mullin, Chris 33–4
Murphy, Michael 129, 163, 164
Myson's factory (Kirkby) 124

National Association of Victim
Support Schemes 102
National Coal Board 32
National Executive Committee
(NEC) 119, 154, 159, 160, 161,
162–3, 166, 167–8, 169
Nellist, David (Militant MP) 75
New Deal for Victims (Penal Affairs
Group) 102
New Statesman 89
News at Ten (ITN) 100, 124–5
News of the World 17, 51, 127
Nicholson, Brian (chairman,
Management Services
Commission) 47
North West Water Authority 78–9
NUM 12–13

Oakes, Gordon (MP for Widnes) 29
Olds, PC 20
Openshaw, Judge 20
Orme, Stan (MP for Salford East)
26–7, 41

Ormkirk constituency 2, 4, 22, 35,
67, 80, 112
Otis Elevator 74, 135
Owen, David 105–6
Owens, Bobby (T & G regional
secretary) 116, 121–2, 135, 137,
149

Page, Anne 134
Parkinson, Cecil 41, 118
Parkinson, Michael and Mary 167
Parry, Bob (MP for Liverpool
Riverside) 3–5, 6, 7, 76, 99
Penal Affairs Group, Parliamentary
20, 70, 90, 101–4, 146, 152
Pendletons Ice Cream factory 135
Penhaligon, David (MP for Truro)
118
Percy, Norma 114
Pimblett, Jack 29, 30
Plead, David 121
Police Review 13, 90, 121, 138, 166,
167
Prescot: unemployment in 44–5
Prescot East Labour Party 132,
154–6, 160
Prescot Labour Club 43, 89, 112
Prescot Museum 142–3
Prescott, John (shadow Employment
Minister) 25, 41
*Prevention of Crime Among Young
People, The* (Penal Affairs Group)
102
Prior Committee 146
Public Order Bill 85
Punch 93

Radical Alternatives to Prison 102
Radice, Giles (shadow Secretary of
State for Education) 69, 70
Radio City (Merseyside) 7–8, 115
Radio Merseyside 115
Rainford, Tony 95
Rayner, Clare 167
Redhead, Brian 122
Rees, Colleen 40
Rees, Merlyn 40
Reid, Lucy 138
Reid, Piers Paul (novelist) 138
Repatriation of Prisoners Act 92

Richardson, Charles 20
Roberts, Allan (MP for Bootle) 73, 76, 129, 134, 141
Roby, Joe 44, 52–4
Rooker, Jeff (MP for Birmingham Perry Bar) 26–7, 28, 34, 41, 70, 148–9
Rumbold, Angela (junior Environment Minister) 78–9
Rutherford, Andrew (lecturer, Southampton University 61

St Paul's, Bristol 107
Sawyer, Tom (deputy general secretary of NUPE) 33
Scargill, Arthur 12–13, 15, 17, 29, 32, 62, 165
SDP 148
Sedgemore, Brian (MP) 105, 162, 165–6
Shaw, Giles (junior Home Office Minister) 107
Sheerman, Barry (MP for Huddersfield) 23, 77, 99
Shore, Peter 67, 70
Silk, Mrs (the author's mother) see Kilroy, Mrs
Silk, Robert (the author's uncle) 127
Silk, William (the author's father) 86–7, 127, 132
Silkin, John (MP for Lewisham) 26–7, 41, 70, 162
Silkin, Sam (now Lord Silkin of Dulwich) 96, 102
Skinner, Dennis 33–4, 41, 45, 71, 105–6
Smith, John (MP) 70
Smith, John (prisoner) 20
Soames, Emma (journalist) 138
Socialist Medical Association 9
Society of Labour Lawyers 9, 76
Spats (the author's duck) 125–6
Stacey, Noni (the author's researcher) 44, 79, 88, 131
Star, The 43, 144
Still Too Many Prisoners (Penal Affairs Group) 101
Stockbridge Village 40, 110
Stonefrost Report 123

Stott, Roger (MP for Westhoughton) 41–2
Strang, Gavin (MP for Edinburgh East) 42
Straw, Jack (MP for Blackburn) 25, 41
Subway (film) 64
Summerskill, Shirley 40
Sun, The 108, 115–16, 118, 122
Sunday Times 127–8
Sydall, Clive 42

TASS (Liverpool North Branch) 91, 97, 100
Tebbitt, Norman 24, 143
Thatcher, Margaret (PM) 44–9, 74, 92, 110, 111, 117, 143
This Week, Next Week (TV programme) 18–19, see also Cockerell, Michael
Thorne, Neil (MP for Ilford South) 71
Time Out 120, 125, 140, 141, 144, 160, 165–6, 167
Times, The 18, 115, 144; articles 6, 97–8, 109, 118, 122, 131–2; letters 106, 109–10, 123, 129–30, 163
Timpson, John 122
Tobacco Workers' Union 57, 97
Today (radio programme) 122–3
Toner, Cathy (Militant Knowsley North constituency secretary) 10–11, 60, 91, 97
Too Many Prisoners (Penal Affairs Group) 101
Tory, Peter 43, 144
Tottenham riots 58–9, 107
Toxteth riots 59
Trades Council 16
Transport and General Workers Union (T & G) 4, 10, 11, 76, 109, 124, 145–6; delegates investigated 16, 21–2, 56–7, 60, 65–6, 116–17, 121–2, 134–6, 137, 142, 149, 161
Trefgarne, Lord (Minister of State for Defence) 109
Tribune Group 41
TUC 12

Turner, Muriel (assistant general
    secretary, ASTMS) 31
TV AM 47, 162–3

UCATT 76
Ullswater, Lord 70
Under Fire (TV programme) 54–5
Utting, David 24, 71–2

Wareing, Bob (MP for Liverpool,
    West Derby) 25–6, 73, 76, 129,
    134
Webster, Philip 115
West, Carol 141
West Lancashire constituency 4, 6
Whitehead, Jean 88–9
Whitehead, Philip 42
Whitelaw, William 24, 54–5, 63
Whitty, Larry 161
Williams, Edna 58, 94, 96
Williams Motors 108–9

Willis, Norman 12
Wilson, Harold 36
Wilson, Woodrow 82
Winnick, David (MP for Walsall
    North) 42
Wogan, Helen 140
Wogan, Terry 140
Women's Council 76
Woods, Clive (Managing Director,
    Mysons) 124
Working Mens College, Camden 106
World at One, The (radio
    programme) 14–15, 24, 32,
    118–20, 141
World in Action 156
Wyatt, Woodrow 127

Ya'acobi, Gad 39
Young, Jimmy 116
*Young Offenders – A Strategy for the
    Future* (Penal Affairs Group) 101